Smuggling Language into the Teaching of Reading

The Charles E. Merrill

COMPREHENSIVE READING PROGRAM

Arthur W. Heilman
Consulting Editor

Smuggling Language into the Teaching of Reading

Arthur W. Heilman
Pennsylvania State University

Elizabeth Ann Holmes
University of Oklahoma

CHARLES E. MERRILL PUBLISHING COMPANY
A Bell & Howell Company
Columbus, Ohio

Published by
Charles E. Merrill Publishing Company
A Bell & Howell Company
Columbus, Ohio

International Standard Book Number: 0–675–09150–0

Library of Congress Catalog Card Number: 72–77393

4 5 6 7 8 9 10 / 76 75

Preface

Smuggling Language into the Teaching of Reading is an outgrowth of several perceptions about reading instruction: First, many children are not learning to read; next, many who do learn are turned away from reading because the experiences associated with learning have curtailed their interest in reading; finally, many teachers admit that *teaching* children to read is often not the exhilarating and rewarding experience it could be.

We can no longer con children into believing that learning to read is a pleasant, rewarding, unmitigated joy if instruction consists of routine uninspiring tasks. Actually, motivating children to read is extremely difficult unless, *while reading*, they are exposed to and develop an appreciation for the power and beauty of language.

This book consists of techniques and procedures for teaching reading as a meaning-making, language-oriented process. It starts from the premise that the activities of teaching and learning can be both fun and growth-provoking. This cannot be achieved by devoting years and years to the teaching of mechanical skills and *then* applying these skills in the reading of "great literature." Very early in their reading careers, children must sense that *all* reading is the "manipulation of language."

Before children can cope with chapters and whole books, they must be taught how to "mine" sentences and brief passages of language. They can be taught *essential skills* while working with these smaller units of reading material. They can be exposed to both the precision and ambiguities of language long before they are exposed to the curriculum of law, medicine, or physics.

While it may be incongruous to talk of smuggling language into reading instruction, the fact remains that children are *not* learning to read. However, children are fascinated by language, and the school should build on this interest. In the final analysis, language is the only magic available in the schools; we hope this handbook will provide some guidelines to help this magic happen.

A. W. H.

E. A. H.

Contents

Reading-and-Writing: Dramatization   69

Study Skills   89

Introduction

Our society places a very high value on "learning to read." We have staked out a period of time in the lives of our children when learning to read takes precedence over every other goal and activity. Children who do not learn to read cannot lead normal lives in our society. Yet, an observer from another planet might conclude that we teach children to read so that it can be said "they have learned how to read."

We would be most reluctant to agree with this analysis, but we do seem a bit hazy as to *why* we are obsessed with teaching every child to read. Some of the more frequently heard reasons are so that children can: get through school; learn about the world around them; make something of their lives; interact with the minds of great poets, statesmen, and thinkers; have access to all the ideas, knowledge, and theories that have ever been written or "stored."

When all the justifications for teaching reading have been catalogued and summated, we end up with a fairly simple statement: We teach children to read so that they have an important *tool for developing and expanding concepts.*

How to Teach Reading is one question we will probably never stop debating. It is possible to teach reading, criticize reading instruction, or even write a book on how to do it without understanding what really goes on during instruction. It is also possible to discover what does go on in reading instruction and be threatened by this discovery.

We have fallen into the habit of thinking that *reading instruction* must surely focus on a global behavior which we call *reading*. From this premise it would follow that when a teacher is teaching reading he is working with a totality—the reading process. While this may be the way we prefer to think about reading instruction, this is not the way it is.

1

Instruction Focuses on Skills

There are approximately 180 school days per year during which blocks of time have been set aside for reading instruction. Observing the real world of the classroom while reading instruction is taking place reveals that instruction always focuses on one or more short-term goals. Each of these short-term goals deals with children mastering some identifiable skill. If one makes an exhaustive list of reading skills, the list will include what the teacher of any given grade will be doing on the 16th, 43rd, or 82nd day of the school year.

Thus, reading instruction deals with fragments of the total process. However, as these somewhat isolated skills are taught, we keep our eyes hopefully on the ultimate goal of instruction, producing critical readers. Actually, there is a problem here that is much more real than it is apparent. A child cannot read something critically if he lacks any essential skill that is required for critical reading. However, since instruction is *skills*-oriented, children often perceive reading as being mechanistic rather than as a language or meaning-making process. Like their elders, they confuse reading with the *activities* associated with learning to read.

These skill-oriented activities are so numerous that several years of instruction are devoted to them. Teaching and reviewing the code-cracking skills can involve so much time and effort that it should be easy to understand why children confuse these activities with reading. The theorist can see that learning hundreds of letter-sound relationships is *in the long run related* to critical reading. But, as week after week is devoted to these isolated teachings, children are justified in concluding that "this is reading."

The worst possible outcome of this type of instruction is that children fail to see reading as language usage. When this occurs, teachers quite frequently end up asking, "How do you motivate children to read?" In other words, it becomes apparent that very few children want to read reading.

Even children who master hundreds of skills, and who in *theory* could mesh all of these skills in critical reading, have little desire to do so. Their experience with *learning to read* has not tied reading to language. Instruction did not provide the proper mix of skills and language usage, and when this component has been neglected, children can easily become reading dropouts even after mastering the mechanics of reading.

Language

Observing the social-intellectual development of children during their first six years, one must be amazed at the role of language in this development. Lately, it has been suggested that educators may be underestimating children's grasp of language. It would also be reasonable to suggest that our instructional strategies in teaching reading ignore the tremendous motivational value that resides in language.

While language is a social tool, it is interesting to note children's language usage in situations where no other individuals are involved. In such situations, children use language with a passion. When a child is alone, he will play two, three, or more roles, each of which involves language. He soon senses that this highly rewarding behavior is perceived by adults as being a bit odd. Gradually the child self-consciously inhibits these double and triple roles when adults invade his life space. He stops talking out loud and conducts his language-play subvocally.

During the late 1960s and early 1970s, there were several television programs in which adults "talked" to child viewers as if they really existed. Such programs often irritate adults, particularly if they have never really observed how children interact in this language situation.

Language and Reading

The power of language for producing growth is greatly diluted when children enter school. Prior to entering school, their language growth was developed both through hearing models and through *use*. The latter would qualify as the true measure of language acquisition. The school, possibly without intention, is structured so that a large part of the child's language experience is passive. Much of the time when language is used, the child functions as a *hearer*, as a consumer rather than as a producer. This enforced passivity tends to inhibit language growth.

In the schools' defense, it might be reasoned that chaos will result in classrooms of 25 pupils if the use of language is not controlled. Perhaps the real issue is whether or not the school's intervention is too abrupt, too thorough, and too rigid. If it is true that spontaneity is stifled, however, then alternatives to present practices should be found.

All teaching done in the school must pass through the language filter before it becomes *learning*. There is quite a loss between teaching input and learning outcome. Recently, having discovered pockets of poverty and ghetto children, we also discovered that the language of the school was not a good vehicle for teaching these children. The language of the school was significantly different from the language these children know and use.

The language used in teaching children to read is also quite remote from their experience. Instruction in reading, with its basals, decoding emphasis, study of "words," repetition, strange alphabets, color coded cardboard stories, and fat cats on mats seem intent on waiving language in teaching reading. Over-dependence on instructional materials which neglect the power of language impairs the effective teaching of reading. Instruction must draw on and extend the rich language background that most children bring to school. Perhaps if we as teachers could take the time to reflect on how our teaching affects children, we might wish to modify some of our procedures.

Language is the only magic available to the school; all the rest is routine, ritual and rote. The magic of language must come through loud and clear in the teaching of reading. If this does not occur, we produce children who may learn the mechanics but whose later behavior gives rise to the question, "How do you motivate children to *read?*"

One need not resort to a total break with tradition or swear eternal hostility to existing instructional materials. The story of Miss Black, which will be briefly touched upon here, illustrates one option that any teacher can exercise.

As a preface to her story, it can be said that Miss Black had a terrible but beautiful experience. It started with a dream, which was unfortunate. The dream was instrumental in the forming of a national association to save America, euphemistically called DDT (Don't Dream—Teach). This association labeled Miss Black's beautiful experience *Black's Bad Dream*. However, in the underground Educational Literature, it became known as *The Permanent Substitute Teacher*.

The Permanent Substitute Teacher

There are some people who say the whole story is fiction. They maintain there never was a Miss Black, she never borrowed the $20, she never ordered a Double Scotch and Lobster dinner. One of the peculiar facets of the case is that the original testimony mysteriously disappeared from The Educational Archives. What the debunkers of the dream do not know, however, is that a copy of the testimony was made, that it fell into the hands of a true believer who turned it over to the Great Pumpkin. The latter will make the report public when he sees fit to do so.

The facts are these. Miss Black was a teacher, the first to admit (to herself) that some days teaching was more of a bore than an unmitigating joy. She had experienced several consecutive months of bad vibrations in her classroom. She borrowed $20 from the Amalgamated Teachers Credit Union and went out on the town.

Whether it was what she ate, drank, or a combination of both, she later that night had a dream (Black's Bad Dream).* In this dream she was confronted by a computer and accused of being a party to poor teaching. As often happens in dreams, she reacted irrationally. She immediately pleaded guilty without consultation with the Teachers Union legal staff. Dreamlike, she thought pleading guilty would be a mitigating circumstance when punishment was meted out. However, it had already been decided that she was to be made an example of, and as punishment she was sentenced to twenty more years of teaching—with the proviso that during this time she was to function as a *Permanent Substitute Teacher!*

Her dream now turned into a nightmare. Monday morning at 7:30, the phone rang, and the computer told Miss Black to report to third grade at Jackson School; Tuesday, it was first grade at Dunbar; Wednesday, sixth grade at Lincoln School; Thursday, back to third grade, but this time at Douglas, and so on for twenty years.

In Miss Black's own handwriting, we are told that she was greatly relieved when she awoke from this bad dream.** In fact she reached a new

* See The Great Pumpkin Papers.
** *See Supplementary Anecdotal Records*, Great Pumpkin Papers, Vol. II.

manic-cycle-high because it was Saturday and tomorrow was Sunday. She didn't have to teach at all for 48 hours!

Just about this time, the insidious aspect of her experience began to take hold of her. She became convinced that the dream was a harbinger. She had been warned in a dream and what had happened in the dream would be fulfilled in real life.

Without knowing why, she suddenly thought of the story of Br'er Rabbit who was destined to receive the worst punishment Ole Bear could think of. "Throw him in the briar patch," said Ole Bear. "You are a permanent substitute teacher," echoed Old Computer. Miss Black recalled that Br'er Rabbit thrived on his punishment—he actually *enjoyed* it. She knew in a flash that this was the key. There must be a way to make being a permanent substitute bearable, maybe even pleasant.

She sat down and tried to recall those days—any day—that teaching had been fun. She wanted some models; what had happened on good days? Obviously, she remembered the day she almost got fired for being a good teacher. The social studies lesson hadn't been very meaty. Something about the Great Southwest with cattle ranches, stockyards, huge herds of cattle, horses, and cowboys. The discussion was over and she knew she needed some filibuster material, so she threw out the question, "What other animals are helpful to man?" The whole thing was just short of dramatic.

Then boom! The one kid she always tried to ignore suggested, "Let's name animals that are smaller than an average-size fox." Before she could suggest that he go to the office, the rest of the class was off and naming. They not only named, they challenged, debated, rebutted, refuted, and modified original stances. It was the phrase "average size" that got things rolling. This was just the right chunk of language to come before fox. The discussion was still in progress when the social studies period ended. As she recalled the situation, she was about to say, "Get out your _____" when someone volunteered "mongoose."

Someone was immediately corrected, "You trying to talk French or something? Who ever heard of a mon—it's *man*, like man goose!" Third girl, second row, chimed in with "you don't go around saying man goose, it's '*drake*.' " Miss Black recalled saying, "Oh, I believe *that's* gander." Willie, the history buff, supported Miss Black saying, "Yeh, Drake was an admiral." The new kid from Iowa insisted Drake was "the relays." The questions, What's an admiral? and What's a relay? were forgotten when original boy said, "No! It's a mongoose! A mongoose is smaller than an average-size fox and it kills cobras."

The room buzzed. An animal smaller than an average-size fox, and it kills cobras. Miss Black recalled saying "children, let's get out our _____." She didn't quite finish because she didn't really have the floor. "Let's look it up, Miss Black." "Can I use the encyclopedia." "Is mongoose in the dictionary— how do you spell it?" Miss Black recalled there was a tide running and she swam with it.

Yes, they could research the mongoose; yes, they could go to the library, read trade books, read animal books, borrow encyclopedias, use the dictionary, gather facts, compare notes, write a story.

Things the class found out: The mongoose is
2 ft. long including the tail
16 inches long
15—18 inches long
"ferret-like"
"weasel-like"
found in India
found in Africa, Asia, especially India
known for a fierce disposition
easy to tame

In addition, the plural of mongoose is mongooses. There are none in the U.S. It is illegal to bring a mongoose or mongooses into the U.S. The mongoose kills cobras, snakes, rats, and as one boy said, Ettkuhs. An Ettkuh is a very hard word to pronounce. It is spelled, etc. Miss Black had to write this on the board: *Etc.* means "and so forth." Everybody learned Etc.

John[2], who used the dictionary to look up mongoose, read a little too much and came up with a riddle: "What's the difference between *money bag* and moneybags?" No one knew; most everyone thought one was singular and the other was plural. John[1] asked John[2] "What *is* the difference between money bag and moneybags?" And John[2] read the definition from the dictionary which temporarily interrupted the discussion of the mongoose. For two weeks anyone who had a nickel or more was "moneybags."

Three children missed the bus. Two mystified parents called the school, "What was going on there today?" "No, no complaints, but Bobby wants a book about the mongoose. Is that a bird that is almost extinct like the whooping crane?" The principal couldn't find the mongoose in the social studies text or basal reader. He said to Miss Black, "May I see your lesson plans for today? What's this about the mongoose? Is that in our curriculum? Do you think we should be discussing the mongoose when the Russians are catching up to us in space?"

It was nice to reminisce, but here it was Saturday, after the Dream. Miss Black had just two days to prepare for her Monday ordeal.

Just then, Pumpelstilskin appeared. He said, "You have a problem. I will show you how to spin gold from straw." She missed the whole point of his proposal as she replied, "I do not need your help, for I have just discovered for myself how you spin gold from straw. You cease to be obsessed with straw and chaff and you let the children spin their soft golden strands of language. Some make golden webs and, some, golden sails for "frigates that bear them lands away." Pumpy said "you are mixing your metaphors," and she replied, "Yes, golden metaphors, similes, ironies, platitudes, and even ettkuhs."

Yes, it was Saturday, and Miss Black had two days in which to prepare for Monday, which she felt certain would be her first day as a Permanent Substitute Teacher. She wondered to which grade the computer would assign her. She suspected it would be first or fourth, since she was presently teaching third.

After recalling the incident of the "smaller than an average-size fox" and the mongoose episode, she began to feel that perhaps she could beat the system. She had to find ways to work with children's language, to use the power of language to harness their egos to learning tasks.

Miss Black prepared a number of riddles, some kernel sentences to be expanded, a number of "fact-or-opinion" sentences, a page of true-false statements that cut across just about everything in the school curriculum, some analogies, and a few proverbs.

Monday morning came. The phone didn't ring. Miss Black reported to her third grade classroom. "What a pity," she thought, "I was so well prepared for first and fourth grade and here I am teaching my own third grade." She thought that after working all weekend she should run, what they call in the trade, a pilot study. She would try using some of the materials she had prepared.

About this time, or a few minutes later, she made a startling discovery. Although she had designed language-reading exercises for other grade levels, it was a simple matter to adapt these materials to her present situation. The exhilarating insight stormed through her insight-center—that by simply adapting materials, she was ready for any grade level that the computer could assign. In addition, she could cope with individual differences found in any classroom.

She had planned to read the riddles to the first graders because they couldn't read them. However, the third graders could read them, so she put her sheet of riddles on the overhead projector. In grade one she had expected to tease out only six or eight different meanings for the word "*set*" (set of dishes, set the table, television set, set your hair, a sunset, a set of numbers, etc). Third graders gave fifteen uses.

Several of the *Fact or Opinion* statements served as the basis for considerable discussion. One which read, "Within ten years the U.S. will have a woman President," triggered a number of comments, mostly from girls:

"Women are smarter than men."
"If George Washington was the father of our country, who was the mother?"
"There are more women voters than men."
"If a woman were president . . ."

Someone (average-size fox, again) pointed out that all of these things didn't fit in the game. Miss Black switched to working with analogies.

Miss Black reached in her purse for a cleansing tissue and pulled out the clipping. Reading the newspaper a few days before the night of the dream, she had run across something on the sports page that puzzled her. It told of one of the "Knicks being closely guarded and eschewing his usual net swishing set shot, used the boards and banked in a tie-breaking two pointer." She had cut this out of the paper intending to have the Junior High Coach explain it to her—hopefully, as he bought her a cup of coffee.

She changed her plans, read this cryptograph to the class, and asked for a translation. A couple of round ball buffs dug the jive and laid it out for her and the rest of the class. They enjoyed the lucid and illustrated explanations of a bank shot. (Someone, again, left his seat and dribbled an imaginary basket-ball close in to the blackboard. His feet left the floor and practically everyone saw the ball hit the board and go through the net, a perfect bank shot.)

You could bank on the fact that this wasn't the end of bank and all of its inflected forms. Different meanings popped up from all parts of the room, and Miss Black put them on the board as fast as she could write: fell in a snow-bank, curves on roads are banked, sat on the river bank, bankers are not the same as basketball players, a bank is a building, I had a bank book, 9 to 3 are banking hours, a blood bank, never bank on the weather. Someone did it again. He came up with, "The guide banked the fire for the night."

This called for an explanation. The explanation led to a discussion of the dangers inherent in the use of fire in forests and woodlands, the damage a recent fire had done in the West (TV), how difficult it was to get a place to camp in national parks. John[2] reported a conversation with a Ranger. John[1] asked, "how many National Parks are there?" and then volunteered, "There are lots of bats in Corl's Bad Tavern."

Miss Black corrected the misconception and said, "Now here are some things we might do." When the principal stuck most of his head in the room, he was pleased and proud. They were reading, they were writing, they were learning, they were enjoying. "What have we going today?" he said. "Why," replied Miss Black, "this is our first annual in-depth study of National Parks and how to preserve them as ecological microcosms for future generations." "Fine, excellent, right on!" said the principal. As he walked down the hall, he toyed with the idea of removing the mongoose entry from Miss Black's folder. She had come a long way since the day she didn't follow her lesson plan.

Miss Black's story is told here because it is believed her experience should not have been labeled a *Bad Dream*. She encouraged children to enjoy language as part of reading instruction, and taught them that they must read *sentences* critically if they wish to read chapters and books that way. Not all of the material that follows comes from Miss Black's teaching file. Some comes from other experienced teachers and some from young people preparing to teach. Many of the techniques have been *adapted* many times. Teachers are encouraged to continue this process.

Intonation
and
Reading

It is essential that children, while learning to read, come to understand that what they read simply represents speech. In speech we use many intonation variations such as:

1. *Stress* or emphasis on a particular word in a sentence.
   (*Really* I am.   Really *I* am.   Really I *am*.)
2. Pauses in the flow of speech (called *junctures* or *terminals*).
   (Indicated in writing by commas, periods, dashes, etc.)
3. Variations in pitch (low, normal, high, etc.). This might be illustrated by a comparison of how one would deliver the following messages.
   - A.   Look at that big oil truck.
   - B.   *Look out* for that truck!

In *A*, the speaker is calling attention to a truck going by.

In *B*, his companion is about to step into the path of the truck.

Printing or writing cannnot convey all of the intonation signals that are used in speech. However, all of the punctuation marks we use do provide clues to intonation or to what is called the "melody of the sentence." For instance, the three different signals at the conclusion of the following sentence do change the melody considerably.

This is your pencil.
This is your pencil?
This is your pencil!

The following exercises focus on the teaching of intonation patterns and the importance of using proper intonation in reading.

Teaching Intonation Using Color
Rhymes and Number Rhymes

PURPOSE: To provide practice in distinguishing *stress* (emphasis) on words in sentences and to develop skill in listening.

PROCEDURE: Explain the task: Children are to listen carefully to each statement. They are to supply (in unison) a color word in the first group of sentences and a number word in the second group that rhymes with the stressed word in each sentence.

1. Purple grass I've never *seen*
    The grass I've seen was mostly _____.   (green)
2. One of the things I like to *do*
    Is color the clouds a nice light _____.   (blue)
3. Mother said, Come and have a *drink*
    I've made some lemonade that's _____.   (pink)
4. The witch had a *sack* upon her *back*
    It wasn't striped—it was solid _____.   (black)
5. I knew two boys named *Ted* and *Fred*
    A funny thing—their hair was _____.   (red)
6. Robert was a handsome *fellow*
    He wore a shirt that was bright _____.   (yellow)
7. I saw a cat the other *day*
    Its eyes were green, its fur was _____.   (grey)
8. If you name a color that rhymes with *man*
    You won't say blue—you must say _____.   (tan)

----

1. I saw a number on the *door*
    The number that I saw was _____.   (four)
2. The snakes I counted in the *den*
    Were more than six, I counted _____.   (ten)
3. The number that will rhyme with *line*
    Is not fourteen, it must be _____.   (nine)
4. This number rhymes with *late* and *gate*
    There's only one and that is _____.   (eight)
5. If I say the color *blue*
    The rhyming number must be _____.   (two)
6. Making rhymes is always *fun*
    To make a rhyme I just say _____.   (one)
7. To keep this rhyming game *alive*
    We have to say the number _____.   (five)
8. Words like *bee* and *tree* and *see*
    Rhyme with good old number _____.   (three)

9. If you're good at doing *tricks*
    You'll make a rhyme by saying _____. (six)

Emphasizing Different Words

Changing Melody of Sentences

PURPOSE: To provide practice in noting how placing emphasis on different words affects the melody and meaning of sentences.

PROCEDURE: Prepare a number of sentences. Write them one at a time on chalkboard. Read the sentence *to* the group and *with* the class. Explain that (1) a question (who-what-when-where-etc.) will be asked; (2) a volunteer will be chosen to read the entire sentence emphasizing the word (or words) that answer the question.

EXAMPLE: *John wants to ride the boat now.*

(Q) Who wants to ride in the boat?
(A) *John* wants to ride the boat now.

(Q) What does John want to ride in?
(A) John wants to ride the *boat* now.

(Q) When does John want to ride?
(A) John wants to ride the boat *now.*

ILLUSTRATIVE SENTENCES:

1. The announcer said it rained hard in Chicago this morning.
2. The train left the station on track three.
3. John found a quarter at the playground.
4. The teacher looked at the picture and said, "good!"
5. There was no game in Chicago because of rain.

VARIATION: Change questions from "who," "what," and "where" to a more general format.

1. Write a sentence on the board.

    The mother robin hopped across the lawn looking for worms.

2. Ask a volunteer to underline the word that shows that the robin . . .
    a. did not fly or run.
    b. was not looking for seeds.
    c. did not hop on the sidewalk.
    d. etc.

PROCEDURE: Prepare a duplicated sheet which shows the same sentence several times but with different words underlined to suggest different intonation patterns. A volunteer selects a group (A to D) and says, "I will read a sentence from group A (B-C-D)." The class (or volunteer) then gives the number of the sentence read, i.e. A-1; A-2; A-3, etc.

A

1. *This* is not my coat.
2. This *is not* my coat.
3. This is not *my coat*.
4. This is not my *coat*.

B

1. The chief died *years* ago.
2. The chief *died* years ago.
3. The chief died years *ago*.
4. The *chief* died years ago.

C

1. This machine will *never* run again.
2. *This* machine will never run again.
3. This machine will never run *again*.
4. This *machine* will never run again.

D

1. "He doesn't deserve to be *elected*," said Fred.
2. "*He* doesn't deserve to be elected," said Fred.
3. "He doesn't *deserve* to be elected," said Fred.
4. "He doesn't deserve to be elected," said *Fred*.

Intonation Expresses Feelings

PURPOSE: To provide practice in noting how different moods or attitudes are suggested by different intonation patterns.

PROCEDURE: Group work, oral presentation. May use chalkboard, overhead projector, or duplicated sheets.

1. Place a number of words on the blackboard, each of which describes a different emotion.

    anger   fright   happiness   surprise   friendliness   sadness

2. Provide a number of sentences. A child volunteers to read a particular sentence.

    a. Put that thing down, Bob.
    b. I want you to listen carefully.
    c. I got this for my birthday.
    d. Which one of you brought the message?
    e. I can't believe it; of course, it's impossible.

3. The volunteer whispers to the teacher the emotion or attitude he intends to illustrate. He reads the sentence and then calls on a volunteer(s) who names the emotion he detected.

Profiting from Punctuation

PURPOSE: To provide practice in noting the role of punctuation marks as they relate to intonation and meaning.

CONCEPTS:

1. How punctuation marks serve as "signals" to indicate *pauses, emphasis,* and *pitch.*
2. How the absence of punctuation may distort meaning in reading.
3. How proper punctuation helps the reader determine meaning.
4. How changes in punctuation influence intonation patterns and meaning.

PROCEDURE:

1. Present introductory material via chalkboard or overhead projector.
2. Use sentence in which the meaning can be altered by changes in punctuation.

EXAMPLES:

1. Father said Jack come and play.
2. "Father" said Jack, "Come and play."
3. Father said, "Jack come and play."

(Discuss changes in intonation and meaning in sentences 2 and 3.)

1. That little boy said his brother is dirty.
2. That little boy, said his brother, "is dirty."
3. That little boy said, "His brother is dirty."

(Discuss differences in intonation and meaning in sentences 1, 2, and 3.)

Changing Meaning

TEACHER: Add punctuation marks to each *sentence B* to change the meaning as found in *sentence A.*

A. This is my brother Tom the football player.
B. This is my brother Tom the football player.

A. The book said the teacher is unimportant.
B. The book said the teacher is unimportant.

A. Your son said his friend is ill.
B. Your son said his friend is ill.

A. Jerry said Mary is always late.
B. Jerry said Mary is always late.

A. All the answers he wrote on the board are wrong.
B. All the answers he wrote on the board are wrong.

Adding Punctuation Marks and Capital Letters

TEACHER: The stories below were written without punctuation marks and capital letters. Put in the punctuation marks and capital letters that are needed to make the stories easy to read.

Story A

After school in the spring my friends and I would often play baseball we would go to the empty lot behind my house when we were finished playing some of my friends would stay for supper we had lots of fun together

Story B

The boy came home right after school his mother gave him some cookies milk and an apple he ate everything he said thank you and went out to play wasn't he a lucky boy

Mixed-up Punctuation

PURPOSE: To provide practice in noting how punctuation helps the reader.

PROCEDURE:

1. Prepare brief paragraphs which include deliberate errors in punctuation and capitalization. Children are to rewrite the passage so that it "makes sense."
2. Explain to students that, "The passage has the punctuation marks and capital letters "mixed up." When these "signals" are wrong, the meaning gets mixed up. Have the children rewrite the paragraph, changing the punctuation and capital letters so that the "signals" help the reader get the meaning.

Billy listened, carefully as the teacher. Explained how punctuation helps. The reader commas periods exclamation marks and question marks? All help a reader get meaning. From the printed page. Billy wondered what would happen. If the printer got the punctuation marks mixed. Up it was hard for him to imagine. What this would do to a story.

Rewrite

_____
_____
_____
_____
_____
_____
_____
_____

Expanding
Word
Meanings

The dual purpose of the school is to help learners develop and expand concepts and develop tools which permit them to do this away from school. The most important growth gradient with which the school deals is the individual's stock of word meanings. The learning goals of each curriculum area are achieved primarily through written or spoken language.

By the time a child encounters formal reading instruction, he has already developed a good command of the mechanics or syntax of his native language. His major learning problem is how many meanings can he program into this syntactical structure. The English speaking child has some 600,000 "words" to draw from and arrange into meaning-bearing units. Obviously, he cannot hope to learn and use more than a small percentage of this vast total. However, the size of his meaning vocabulary will determine to a large degree the things he can and cannot do in his language-oriented society.

Expansion of word meanings depends on experience with language. The exercises in this unit attempt to guide the learner in mastering word meanings and also important facts *about* his language such as:

1. A given word may have many different meanings.
2. Words may be pronounced the same and have different meanings.
3. *Different words* may have much the same meaning, yet the differences are important.
4. Words may have both a more or less fixed meaning and "special meanings" (figurative expressions).

It should be remembered that a particular exercise may present material at one level of difficulty, but this same approach can be used at any level.

Expansion of Meanings

Different Connotations for the Same Word

PROCEDURE:

1. Select a common word that has many different meanings.
2. Explain that the purpose of the activity is to use this word in sentences and that each sentence volunteered should use the word *so that it conveys a meaning that is different from any used previously.*
3. A child volunteers when he is ready to supply a sentence.

EXAMPLE: Place on the chalkboard the word *set.* Call for sentences which meet above criteria.

Following are some examples of different meanings for the word *set:*

set the table	ready, get *set*, go
the sun *set*	the *set* in a ring
set of dishes	member of the *Jet set*
set the clock	*set* in mathematics
a television *set*	very *set* in one's ways
a *set* of tennis	the bidder went *set*

FURTHER EXAMPLES: Common words which have many meanings—*light, fine, air, mine, fence, press, match, ball, cool, handle, free, head, miss, fly.*

ILLUSTRATION FOR LIGHT: one may *light* a fire; turn on a *light;* wait for *daylight;* wear a *light-colored* suit or *light-weight* shoes; enjoy a *light meal;* or get caught in a *light rain.*

ILLUSTRATION FOR BANKED: The old scout *banked* the fire. The storekeeper *banked* the day's receipts. The curves on the new highway were well *banked.* He had *banked* on his friend's help. The player *banked* the ball off the backboard into the basket.

Completion Items

TEACHER: "Read the sentences below and fill in each blank with one of the words *can, air,* or *fence* to make the sentences correct."

1. "Don't _____ me in," sang the Cowboy.
2. Johnny went to the store for a _____ of peaches.
3. Mother put the rug on the porch to _____.
4. Our yard is enclosed with a six foot _____.
5. Mother will _____ the fruit for next winter.

TEACHER: "Fill the blanks with the appropriate word, *mine*, *blue*, or *horse*."

1. My father worked in the coal _____.
2. I can ride a _____.
3. The dress was _____.
4. "This book is not _____," said Jim.
5. Mary said she felt _____.
6. "When you work, don't _____ around," said Father.

TEACHER: "Read the sentences below and write in your own words a meaning that fits the underlined word."

1. The secretary read the report from the last meeting.

   _____

2. We heard a loud report as the motorcycle passed.

   _____

3. The spider crawled under the board.

   _____

4. The school board held an election last week.

   _____

5. The third graders were adding three column problems.

   _____

6. A large cement column held up the front porch roof.

   _____

Matching Exercise

TEACHER: "Read the sentences in column A. In the blank before the word in column B, write the number of the sentence whose underlined word has the same meaning as the word in column B."

A		B
1. Mary was feeling blue.	_____a.	Discussion
2. The sky was a bright blue.	_____b.	Curtain
3. The Girl Scouts presented a panel on "Safety."	_____c.	Unhappy
	_____d.	Preserve
4. At the window she hung a red and white panel.	_____e.	Color
	_____f.	Container
5. He opened a can of peaches.		
6. The lady will can the fruit.		

Writing Exercise

TEACHER: From the list of words below, write as many sentences with different meanings as you can using the same word.

air   blue   can   horse   mine   fence

Arriving at Word Meanings

PURPOSE: To teach–test the meaning of words found in sentences which provide no clues to the word meaning.

PROCEDURE:

1. Develop a series of sentences each of which contains one or more words which are fairly difficult for the participants. The sentence context should not supply clues to the word meanings. The sample sentences below use terms found in intermediate grade textbooks.
2. Children read each sentence and decide whether the statement is true or false. If material is presented as seatwork, the child places a T or an F in front of each sentence.

PRESENTATION: Material may be presented via the chalkboard, overhead projector, tape recorder,* or duplicated work sheet.

_____ 1.   Wool and leather are examples of *synthetic* materials.
_____ 2.   A *ravine* is a narrow, steep-sided valley.
_____ 3.   *Barnacles* are special stalls for holding milking cows in dairy barns.
_____ 4.   *Irrigation* is commonly used to prepare a swamp for cultivation.
_____ 5.   A *glacier* is a huge mass of ice.
_____ 6.   Snow and hail are examples of *precipitation*.
_____ 7.   The terms *plateau* and *butte* describe the same land formation.
_____ 8.   A *century* is equal to ten *decades*.
_____ 9.   The terms *mammoth*, *immense*, and *huge* are synonyms.
_____10.   A highly skilled person with much experience is called an *apprentice*.

Arriving at Sentence Meaning

PROCEDURE: Same as for Arriving at Word Meanings.

Concepts from Arithmetic

_____ 1.   The sum of two odd numbers is always an odd number.
_____ 2.   No whole number multiplied by itself can equal nine.
_____ 3.   All numbers ending in zero are divisible by ten, five, and two.
_____ 4.   The three measures—6 feet, 72 inches, and 2 yards—are equal.
_____ 5.   Twenty-two ounces equals a pound and one-half.
_____ 6.   Five decades equal one-half century.
_____ 7.   All triangles contain at least one right angle.
_____ 8.   To cut a 20 foot pole into 5 foot lengths, you must saw the pole four times.

* If tape recorder is used, the voice clearly identifies each stimulus statement as Sentence one; Sentence two, etc. Before beginning the exercise, each child numbers a piece of scratch paper to coincide with the number of sentences on the tape. After each number he writes T or F.

_____ 9. A square has four sides that are equal and contains four angles that are equal.

_____10. One and one-quarter hours equals 80 minutes.

Concepts from Social Studies

_____ 1. A *lagoon* is an animal found in the tropics or other warm climate.

_____ 2. An *island* must be surrounded by water.

_____ 3. Man-made materials are called *synthetics*.

_____ 4. A *serf* is one who makes his living off the sea.

_____ 5. A high mountain peak is called a *ravine*.

_____ 6. *Sorghum* looks like corn and is used as a feed for animals.

_____ 7. *Irrigation* is a method used by farmers to drain flooded farmland or swampy area.

_____ 8. An *immigrant* is a person who leaves his home and settles in a new country.

_____ 9. "Fallow fields" are fields which do not have crops planted in them.

_____10. If a nation has a *low literacy rate*, most of its people can read and write.

Defining Words

PURPOSE: To provide practice in working with difficult words in sentence contexts.

PROCEDURE: Prepare materials similar to samples below. The pupil writes his own definition of the underlined word. If he feels his knowledge of the word is hazy or incomplete, he may add the dictionary definition. Group discussion of items should follow use of the exercise. This helps to clear up misconceptions and helps children "use" the words.

1. John was in a <u>quandry</u>, as he listened to the engineers report.
    (mine)_____
    (dictionary) _____
2. As she talked, you could tell she was filled with <u>conceit</u>.
    (mine)_____
    (dictionary) _____
3. His interest in reading was <u>dormant</u> for a long time.
    (mine)_____
    (dictionary) _____
4. The family embarked on a <u>perilous</u> journey.
    (mine)_____
    (dictionary) _____
5. The driver had trouble with <u>parallel</u> parking.
    (mine)_____
    (dictionary) _____

6. Her attempt to <u>feign</u> illness was not successful.
(mine)_____
(dictionary) _____

Working with Relationships

Relationship

TEACHER: "Each word in column **A** can be associated with one word in column **B**. Draw lines connecting the appropriate words in **A** to those in **B**."

A	B	A	B
clock	milk	rat	calf
cow	boat	fish	swim
paper	time	cow	cat
lake	tire	frog	comb
car	pencil	rooster	hop

A	B	A	B
coffee	library	zoo	snow
trip	cup	calender	bags
book	bat	winter	dates
ocean	map	shirt	giraffe
baseball	beach	tea	tie

A	B	A	B
snow	read	spelling	words
color	water	trunk	thread
newspaper	red	spool	coat
island	sled	cowboy	elephant
telephone	ring	hat	horse

Classifying

PROCEDURE: Use the chalkboard to explain the activity. Place a series of words on the board (there may be 3-, 4-, or 5-word series). All but one of the words fit into a particular grouping (food, animals, plants, games, etc.). The reader must determine the attribute which is common to all but one of the stimulus words and identify the *one* word which does not belong in the group.

PRESENTATION: Material may be presented via the chalkboard, overhead projector, or duplicated materials.

TEACHER: "In the blank spaces, write the word which does not belong in the series."

1. fish, frog, pond, bird   _____
2. copper, lead, pottery, tin   _____

    3. cornflakes, carrots, potatoes, beans   —————
    4. hat, wagon, coat, shoes   —————
    5. chalk, blackboard, paper, notebook   —————
    6. center, tackle, shortstop, guard   —————
    7. spade, hoe, rake, hammer   —————
    8. New Mexico, Mexico, New Jersey, Ohio   —————
    9. know, knight, knee, kite   —————
   10. summer, cold, hot, warm   —————

Analogies

PURPOSE: To develop critical reading-thinking skills through practice in seeing relationships such as:

   1. Part to whole ("finger is to hand as toe is to foot")
   2. Function ("shoe is to foot as glove is to hand")

PRESENTATION: Materials may be presented in different ways such as via chalkboard, overhead projector, or duplicated sheets for individualized work.

TEACHER: "Complete the following analogies by underlining the one word on the right that completes the sense of the statement. Be alert for relationships such as 'part to the whole' and 'function.'"

   1. Ship is to navy as tank is to   swimmer   automobile   army
   2. Bread is to butter as cracker is to   box   cheese   diet
   3. Glove is to hand as sock is to   boot   shoe   foot
   4. Red is to sweater as blue is to   shirt   ocean   topaz
   5. Up is to down as over is to   there   under   upper
   6. Bullet is to gun as arrow is to   bow   quiver   target
   7. Good is to bad as down is to   under   up   over
   8. Robin is to bird as mosquito is to   insect   fly   net
   9. Orange is to fruit as carrot is to   stew   vegetables   food
  10. Minute is to hour as second is to   first   hour   minute

TEACHER: "Circle the word in column **B** that will fit with the series of words in column **A**."

	A	**B**
1.	dog, cat, rat	bird snake rabbit
2.	girl, boy, man	house woman car
3.	dress, hat, coat	shoe chair table
4.	kitten, calf, puppy	horse colt lion
5.	lion, tiger, elephant	giraffe pencil box
6.	Spring, Summer, Autumn	hat cold Winter
7.	watch, earrings, ring	necklace comb brush

8. pencil, paper, book	radio ruler roof
9. pitcher, catcher, batter	quarterback first-baseman tackle
10. pretty, ugly, sweet	sour fly run

TEACHER: "Draw a line from the word in column A to the series it completes in column B."

A	B
gnat	orange, banana
apple	fly, mosquito
chair	mail, post office
spoon	table, bed
letter	knife, fork

A	B
pencil	bicycle, train
brick	tablet, chalk
truck	bag, carton
box	encyclopedia, atlas
dictionary	stone, concrete

Figurative Expressions

The English language is rich with figurative expressions and idiomatic phrases. These occur with high frequency even in the materials prepared for use in the elementary grades. Since children are likely to think in terms of literal meanings, they need practice in reading such expressions, discussing their meanings, and in using them in their own speech and writing.

Recognizing Expressions

PROCEDURE: Have children underline the sentence in each group that contains a figurative expression. Then, in group work, identify the expressions, discuss their meanings, and devise other ways of "saying it."

1. Mary went to the store.
Mary saw a pretty doll.
Mary's eyes sparkled with delight when she saw the doll.

2. The airplane soared into the wild blue yonder.
The airplane flew very high in the sky.
The airplane flew over the city.

3. The boy is a good swimmer.
He jumped off the diving board and sailed gracefully into the pool.
He swims every day in the summer.

4. My father has a new car.
    My father drives his car to work.
    My father took off like a bullet as he left for work.

5. We had a test in class today.
    We had to put on our thinking caps to pass the test.
    We had lots of questions on the test.

6. The weather was very cold.
    Snowflakes danced and swirled across the yard.
    Everyone remained in the house.

7. Everyone was angry with Tim.
    Many tried to keep him from succeeding.
    Tim counted every knock as a stepping-stone to success.

TEACHER: "Read the following sentences. Write 'yes' in the blank before each sentence that contains a figurative expression. Write the figurative expression from each sentence marked 'yes' on the line below the sentence."

_____ 1.   Her behavior takes the cake.

_____

_____ 2.   The car was parked near the curb.

_____

_____ 3.   A policeman has to keep on his toes to keep up with criminals.

_____

_____ 4.   The judge asked the witness a question that put her on the spot.

_____

_____ 5.   The new submarine was watertight.

_____

_____ 6.   The ship stopped at many ports.

_____

_____ 7.   They like to travel on the train.

_____

_____ 8.   Answering the question backed him into a corner.

_____

_____ 9.   My grandfather would always spin us a yarn before we went to bed.

_____

_____10.   After the storm the sun broke through the clouds.

_____

Completion Exercise

TEACHER: "Fill blanks in column **A** with the word from column **B** that completes the figurative expression."

A

1. Her eyes sparkled like _____.
2. The wind was _____ down the street.
3. Trouble seemed to _____ his footsteps.
4. The pilot completed the first _____ of the journey.
5. The boy was as stubborn as a _____.
6. Nobody trusted him because he was a _____ in the grass.

B

1.	dog	5.	leg
2.	mule	6.	snake
3.	roar	7.	diamonds
4.	howling		

A

1. The captain's voice blasted out with a loud _____.
2. The girl has the temper of a _____.
3. He was as hungry as a _____.
4. Losing her ticket put her in a terrible _____.
5. "His check is as good as _____," said the banker.
6. The boss said, "Tom, you're as fit as a _____."

B

1.	spitfire	5.	roar
2.	bear	6.	fix
3.	gold	7.	mouse
4.	fiddle		

A

1. Hearing the good news made her as happy as a _____.
2. "We'll be lucky to _____ this storm," said the captain.
3. "A penny for your _____," said mother.
4. When you are angry be careful not to lose your _____.
5. He was so frightened, that he turned as white as a _____.
6. Wearing a suit and tie to the picnic, John stuck out like a sore _____.

B

1.	weather	5.	thoughts
2.	head	6.	lark
3.	thumb	7.	tune
4.	sheet		

Interpreting Common Expressions

PROCEDURE: Prepare sentences each of which contains a common expression. The sentences do not contain clues to the meaning of the expression. Children explain in their own words what these expressions mean.

PRESENTATION: Material may be presented orally, via the chalkboard or over-head projector, or duplicated in the form of worksheets for individual work.

TEACHER: "Read each sentence. Then, write in your own words what the underlined words mean."

1. Grandfather said, "Take your time, Tim, take your time."

   _____

2. After the accident Carl mended his ways.

   _____

3. The police are hot on the trail of the bandits.

   _____

4. John was mad but he managed to hold his tongue.

   _____

5. "I don't dig that jive," said Al.

   _____

6. John lost his head and threw the ball to the wrong base.

   _____

7. "What a game," said Phil. "That was a close shave."

   _____

8. Asked about the quarterback, the coach said, "He's fit as a fiddle."

   _____

9. "Jane nearly bit my head off," said Alice.

   _____

10. The field was alive with grasshoppers.

   _____

   ———————————

TEACHER: "Underline the figurative expressions in each sentence, then tell, in your own words, what the expression means."

1. The wind came howling down the street.

   _____

2. Mary's eyes sparkled like diamonds as she talked.

   _____

3. Willie Mays always hits the ball on the nose.

   _____

4. She liked the dress as soon as she set eyes on it.

    _____

5. The children grew up and scattered to the four winds.

    _____

6. The making of paper was one of the marks of civilization.

    _____

7. The messenger ran with the speed of light.

    _____

8. Boston harbor is primarily the gateway of New England.

    _____

9. Chicago is one of the great crossroads of our country.

    _____

10. Conservation can be called an eye to the future.

    _____

Matching Meanings

PROCEDURE: Prepare a number of sentences each of which contains an underlined expression. Write several statements beneath each sentence. Pupils identify the statement that explains the meaning of the expression.

1. My sister is as <u>pretty as a picture</u>.
    a.   my sister is always very still.
    b.   my sister is very pretty.
    c.   my sister looks like her picture.

2. The pioneers <u>pushed over the mountains</u> to settle the West.
    a.   The pioneers knocked down the mountains to settle the West.
    b.   The pioneers pushed the mountain over with their strength.
    c.   The pioneers crossed the mountains to settle the West.

3. Pittsburgh is <u>the gateway</u> to the mid-west.
    a.   There is a large gate through which people pass to the Midwest.
    b.   People frequently pass through Pittsburgh going to the Midwest.
    c.   Pittsburgh has a large gateway.

4. Her parents were <u>beside themselves</u> with worry.
    a.   Her parents were very worried.
    b.   Her parents stood beside each other and worried.
    c.   Worry was always beside her parents.

5. As soon as school is out the pupils <u>make tracks</u> for home.
    a.   Pupils go home as soon as school is out.
    b.   Pupils draw footprints as soon as school is out.
    c.   Pupils go by the railroad tracks as soon as school is out.

6. In the fall of the year the forest <u>is painted</u> with many colors.
   a. Many people paint the forest in the fall.
   b. Leaves on the trees have many colors in the fall.
   c. Fairies paint the forest in the fall.

7. Mary couldn't <u>make heads or tails</u> of the map.
   a. Mary couldn't understand the map.
   b. Mary tried to draw heads and tails on the map.
   c. Mary couldn't find pictures of heads or tails on the map.

8. The stock car racer <u>took off like a bullet.</u>
   a. The racer took off with a loud noise.
   b. The racer took off very fast.
   c. The racer took off in a straight line.

9. Louise's father <u>gave John her hand.</u>
   a. Louise's father consented to her marriage with John.
   b. Louise's father placed her hand in John's hand.
   c. Louise's father cut her hand off and gave it to John.

10. Do not let your friends <u>stand in your way.</u>
    a. Do not let your friends stand in front of you.
    b. When walking with friends do not let them stand in front of you.
    c. Do not let friends keep you from doing something you want to do.

Key: 1–b, 2–c, 3–b, 4–a, 5–a, 6–b, 7–a, 8–b, 9–a, 10–c

Working with Terms Associated with Sports

PURPOSE: To provide practice in:

1. Reading special terms.
2. Associating these with a particular sport.
3. Writing the meaning for these terms.
4. Creative writing which includes a number of special terms.

PROCEDURE: Place several terms on the chalkboard ("no hitter," "goalie," etc.). Call on individuals to identify the sport in which these terms might be used and to explain what the term means.

———————————

PROCEDURE: Prepare a duplicated exercise similar to those shown below. Exercises may deal with terms usually associated with one sport at a time (i.e., baseball or football).

TEACHER: "Can you identify the sport or game with which each of these terms is associated?

1. On the line following each term, write the name of the sport in which the term might be used.
2. On the line provided below the term explain what the term means."

1. "end zone" ☐ _____
    _____
2. "triple play" ☐ _____
    _____
3. "traveling" ☐ _____
    _____
4. "net ball" ☐ _____
    _____
5. "fair catch" ☐ _____
    _____
6. "penalty box" ☐ _____
    _____
7. "lead off man" ☐ _____
    _____
8. "fast break" ☐ _____
    _____
9. "tenth frame" ☐ _____
    _____
10. "take down" ☐ _____
    _____

PURPOSE: To write stories or paragraphs which include a number of sports terms. The writer should underline each example of such terms.

PROCEDURE: Have children write brief paragraphs on any sport they choose. Encourage use of figurative terms.

EXAMPLE: Randy Phillips, the ace second sacker and lead off man for the visiting club, came to the plate in the first of the third. He promptly looped a blooper into left center which fell in for a two bagger. Later he crossed the plate on a scratch single by Andrews.

Interpreting Idioms and Proverbs

PURPOSE: To provide experience in arriving at the non-literal meaning of brief statements.

PROCEDURE:

1. Prepare a list of proverbs or "sayings" that are at the appropriate difficulty level for the class.
2. Type these (one to a card) on 3 × 5 cards. The cards are placed face down on the desk. A volunteer draws a card, reads the proverb

to the group, and explains its meaning. (Discussion and questions may follow each item.)

1. You never miss the water until the well runs dry.
2. A bird in the hand is worth two in the bush.
3. You can't judge a book by the cover.
4. Don't count your chickens before they hatch.
5. The early bird catches the worm.
6. Always look before you leap.
7. Every cloud has a silver lining.
8. Misery loves company.
9. A stitch in time saves nine.
10. Necessity is the mother of invention.

VARIATIONS:
1. The material may be placed on transparency sheets and used with the overhead projector.
2. Duplicate a sheet of expressions, leaving space following each item for pupils to write the meanings.

Words Often Confused

PURPOSE: To provide practice in working with words that look and sound very much alike and whose meanings are often confused.

TEACHER: "Study the words and definitions in the box. Then, in the sentences below, fill in the blanks with the proper word."

alter:	to change or modify
altar:	place used in worship
medal:	a decoration awarded for service
meddle:	to interfere
cite:	to quote, or use as illustration
sight:	to see, act of seeing
site:	location
council:	a governing group
counsel:	to advise
affect:	to influence
effect:	a result produced by a cause
pitcher:	container for water/a ball player
carton:	a box or container
cartoon:	a drawing, a caricature

meddle–medal   1. It might be a good idea to give a _____ to people who never _____ in others affairs.

alter–altar   2. In over 500 years, no attempt had been made to _____ the _____.

carton–cartoon

counsel–council

3. You will find a humorous _____ on every _____ of breakfast food.

sight–site

4. He hoped to catch _____ of the _____ where the new club was to be built.

counsel–council

5. The city _____ decided to hire an expert to _____ them on this matter.

TEACHER: "The meanings of the pairs of words which follow are not given above. Place the proper word in the blanks in each sentence. Use a dictionary if you are doubtful about the meaning of any word."

miner–minor

1. Most states have laws which prohibit a _____ from working as a _____.

course–coarse

2. The fairways of the golf _____ were covered with _____ grass.

dairy–diary

3. During the day Bill worked in a _____, but each night he would write in his _____.

descend–decent

4. We should try to find a _____ trail if we hope to _____ the mountain before dark.

precede–proceed
cannon–canyon

5. When an army is to _____ through a _____ surrounded by the enemy, it is the usual custom to have a barrage by _____ _____ the march.

TEACHER: "Fill the blanks with the correct word from the box. Use a dictionary, if necessary, to get the correct meaning."

alter	through	medal	site
altar	thorough	meddle	sight

1. The seamstress will _____ her dress.
2. Everyone knelt before the _____.
3. The man was losing his _____.
4. The housing _____ was near the factory.
5. John received a _____ for his bravery.
6. The girl was shunned because she liked to _____ in other peoples' affairs.
7. The librarian was very _____ as she looked _____ the stack of books.

TEACHER: "Read the selection below. Fill the blanks with words from the box that will make the selection meaningful. (Use a dictionary if there is any doubt about the meaning of a word.)"

accept—except	farther—further	advise—advice
quiet—quite	device—devise	whether—weather

The science class was debating w_____ to discuss the local w_____. Some children wanted to do f_____ study and include places that were much f_____ away.

Someone suggested that they d_____ some d_____ for measuring the amount of rainfall. John said, "I a_____ that we seek some a_____ on this matter.

The children were not too q_____ during their planning as they found that they couldn't q_____ decide on all of the details. At the close of the class all e_____ two pupils were willing to a_____ the plans that had been developed.

TEACHER: "In the space provided, write a sentence in which you use the word at the left."

1. metal: _____
2. medal: _____
3. dairy: _____
4. diary: _____
5. miner: _____
6. minor: _____
7. affect: _____
8. effect: _____
9. cereal: _____
10. serial: _____
11. accept: _____
12. except: _____

Working with Homographs

PURPOSE: To develop the concept that some words are spelled exactly alike but have different pronunciations and meanings.

PROCEDURE: Write a common homograph on the board (wind, read, live, etc.). Discussion will establish that the word has two pronunciations and meanings. Illustrate this with sentences.

"They heard the *wind* howling through the trees."
"Remember to *wind* the clock."

Explain that the way in which a word is used in a sentence determines its meaning and pronunciation (at certain instructional levels, it is not necessary to explain the parts-of-speech function, i.e., wīnd—verb; wĭnd—object or noun).

PRESENTATION: Material may be presented via the chalkboard or overhead projector for class discussion, or by means of duplicated work sheets for individual work.

TEACHER: "Some words are spelled alike and yet have different pronunciations and meanings. These words are called homographs. The *context* or 'how the word is used' gives us a clue as to the word's meaning and pronunciation.

Many small farms pro duce' a variety of pro' duce.

The stimulus word which precedes each sentence can be used in both blank spaces. The pronunciation and meaning will be different in each case. Indicate the pronunciation by marking either the vowel sound, *līve, lĭve;* or the accent, *ob'ject, ob ject'*."

live: 1. He was lucky to _____ after touching the _____ wire.

present: 2. The Mayor hoped to be _____ in person to _____ the Citizenship Awards.

object: 3. The teacher will not _____ if we bring this type of _____ to class.

close: 4. The announcer said, "Thus, we _____ this broadcast of a very _____ game."

read: 5. After you _____ a book, you may say you have _____ it.

excuse: 6. The coach would not _____ a player from practice unless he had a good _____.

extract: 7. He had to _____ the cork from the bottle of _____.

tear: 8. When she saw the _____ in her new dress, a _____ came to her eye.

contract: 9. The _____ stated that the material would not _____ when wet.

address: 10. He consented to make the _____ before he obtained the _____ of the meeting place.

ALTERNATIVE APPROACH: Have pupils write sentences which include a stimulus word. "Write a sentence which includes the word on the left."

re fuse'   _____
ref'use   _____
re cord'   _____
rec'ord   _____
lĕad   _____
lēad   _____
sub'ject   _____
sub ject'   _____

Working with Prefixes and Suffixes

PURPOSE: To provide practice in building words by adding affixes.

PROCEDURE: Duplicate sheets of exercises and let pupils fill in the blanks with a prefix or suffix to form a word that fits the definition. (The following exercises have the affixes listed. These should be left off the pupils' exercise sheets.)

to bring into a country	_____port	(im)
to carry	_____port	(trans)
a gate or door	port_____	(al)
sell in another country	_____port	(ex)
bus, train, plane, or car	_____port_____	(trans) (ation)

to not trust	_____trust	(dis)
relying upon	trust_____	(ing)
worthy of trust	trust_____	(worthy)

to no longer continue	_____continue	(dis)
without interruption	continue_____	(ous)
not connected, broken	_____continue_____	(non) (ous)
to work with	_____operate	(co)
a surgical procedure	operate_____	(tion)
not working	_____operate_____	(in) (tive)
after surgery	_____operate_____	(post) (tive)

to take out and replant	_____plant	(trans)
large southern estate	plant_____	(ation)
placed well within	_____plant	(im)
one who sows seeds	plant_____	(er)
placing seeds in the ground	plant_____	(ing)

to look forward to	_____spect	(ex)
to feel or show honor or esteem for	_____spect	(re)
to look into, examine	_____spect	(in)
an onlooker	spect_____	(ator)
to meditate or ponder	spect_____	(ulate)

to play over	_____play	(re)
to show	_____play	(dis)
full of fun	play_____	(ful)
a person who plays	play_____	(er)
it can be played	play_____	(able)

_____

to quit, to stop, to withdraw	_____tire	(re)
exhausted	tire_____	(d)
requiring little rest	tire_____	(less)
not exhausted	tire_____	(some)

_____

to compel	_____force	(en)
strong, powerful	force_____	(ful)
without force	force_____	(less)
to strengthen or make strong	_____ _____force	(re) (in)

Prefixes: Changing Meanings

PURPOSE: To provide practice in noting the changes in word meanings that are achieved by adding prefixes.

PROCEDURE: Add each of the prefixes in the boxes to the words below the box. Then write the definition of the words that were formed.

$$\boxed{\text{mono} - \text{bi} - \text{tri}}$$

_____cycle = _____
_____cycle = _____
_____cycle = _____

$$\boxed{\text{pre} - \text{dis} - \text{re}}$$

_____arrange = _____
_____arrange = _____
_____arrange = _____

$$\boxed{\text{im} - \text{ex} - \text{trans} \qquad (\textit{port} = \text{to carry})}$$

_____port = _____
_____port = _____
_____port = _____

$$\boxed{\text{un} - \text{inter} - \text{re}}$$

_____lock = _____
_____lock = _____
_____lock = _____

$$\boxed{\text{post} - \text{pre} - \text{pro} - \text{anti}}$$

_____war = _____
_____war = _____
_____war = _____
_____war = _____

Working with Synonyms

PURPOSE: To emphasize that different words may have much the same meaning, and to provide practice in working with synonyms.

PROCEDURE: Through group discussion define the term synonym, ask for examples, write some of these on chalkboard.

PRESENTATION: Materials may be presented orally, via overhead projector, or as duplicated exercises.

TEACHER: Write a word in column **B** that means the same or nearly the same as the word in column **A**.

	A	B		A	B
1.	right	_____	1.	bright	_____
2.	above	_____	2.	friendly	_____
3.	chase	_____	3.	cruel	_____
4.	dark	_____	4.	gay	_____
5.	sad	_____	5.	leap	_____
6.	beautiful	_____	6.	awful	_____
7.	unpleasant	_____	7.	smile	_____
8.	clever	_____	8.	swift	_____
9.	wealthy	_____	9.	brave	_____
10.	tidy	_____	10.	timid	_____

Synonym Bingo (two or more players)

PROCEDURE:

1. Make several "bingo cards" (see illustration). These can be 9, 12, or 25 squares according to the difficulty level desired. (Cards should show some variance in words used, word arrangement or both.)

2. Make a list of "pairs of words" or synonyms.

> correct – right
>
> run   – chase
>
> rich   – wealthy
>
> baby   – infant

3. Teacher (or child who knows all the words used) reads a word from the list. Players look for and cover the synonym shown on the card. Decide rules for winning.

← 16 squares to a card →

Right	Beautiful	Bright	Brave	Leap
Above	Unpleasant	Friendly	Swift	Awful
Chase	Clever	Cruel	Tale	Infant
Wealthy	Dark	Gay	Smile	Lead
Sad	Tidy	Astonished	Sick	Tall

(left side: 9 squares to a card)

← 25 squares to a card →

Crossword Puzzles (Synonyms)

TEACHER: Synonyms are words that have the same or nearly the same meaning. Work the puzzle using snyonyms.

¹S	M	³I	L	⁵E	■	⁷G	L	A	D
W	■	L	■	S	■	■	■	■	■
⁹I	L	L	■	¹²C	O	U	P	¹⁶L	E
F	■	■	■	A	■	■	■	E	■
¹⁷T	R	A	M	P	■	■	²²L	A	D
■	■	■	■	E	■	²³M	A	D	■
¹⁸T	A	L	L	■	¹⁹L	■	B	■	²⁰L
A	■	■	■	■	O	■	O	■	E
L	■	■	²¹R	I	V	E	R	■	A
²⁴E	V	E	N	■	E	■	■	■	P

Across

1. grin
7. happy
9. sick
12. two
17. hobo
18. high
21. stream
22. boy
23. upset
24. smooth

Down

1. fast
3. sick
5. flee
16. guide
18. story
19. affection
20. jump
22. work

Working with Antonyms

PURPOSE: To develop and expand concepts through working with words which have opposite meanings.

PROCEDURE: Explain that the term *antonym* means "words that have opposite meanings." Ask for examples and discuss.

NOTE: After children complete an exercise such as the one that follows, discuss their responses with the whole group. It is likely that there will be differences in responses and noting these differences will also help to expand concepts.

TEACHER: "Fill the blank with a word that means the opposite of the word in parenthesis below the blank."

1. Mary bought a _____ dress.
    (old)
2. We _____ from the lion.
    (walked)
3. Goldilocks thought father bear's porridge was too _____.
    (cold)
4. The automobile was going very _____.
    (slow)
5. The ball was lost in the _____ weeds.
    (low)
6. They climbed _____ to the top of the mountain.
    (down)
7. The troops crossed _____ the bridge.
    (under)
8. Always look both ways _____ you cross the street.
    (after)
9. Mother left the light _____ in the bedroom.
    (off)
10. I like to swim in the _____.
    (winter)

TEACHER: "Fill in the blank with the antonym (a word opposite of the word in parenthesis below the blank)."

1. The painting was very _____.
    (ugly)
2. The dog had a very _____ tail.
    (long)
3. The soldier was a very _____ man.
    (cowardly)
4. She always has a _____ on her face.
    (frown)
5. The children like to play _____.
    (indoors)
6. The dove is the symbol of _____.
    (war)
7. Jim _____ his football.
    (found)
8. The pep squad cheered _____ the team.
    (against)
9. My friend moved to a _____ away land.
    (near)
10. An island is land completely surrounded by _____.
    (land)

Crossword Puzzles (Antonyms)

TEACHER: "Antonyms are words with opposite meanings. Work the puzzles using antonyms."

		Across	
1.	end	7.	close
8.	fast	12.	angel
15.	stop	18.	woman
21.	dim	22.	wrong
25.	fat	26.	push

Across

1. end
7. close
8. fast
12. angel
15. stop
18. woman
21. dim
22. wrong
25. fat
26. push

Down

3. bad
5. yes
6. off
8. winter
11. dry
16. in
17. south
21. end
23. hers
24. bottom

¹B	O	³T	T	⁵O	M		⁸O	U	¹⁰T
I		H		N					O
G		I				²⁷S			P
		³³N	I	³⁵G	H	T		³⁹F	
⁴¹U	P			I		A		A	
				R		⁵⁷Y	E	S	
⁶¹S		⁶³W	A	L	K			⁶⁹T	⁷⁰O
L									P
⁸¹O	F	F			⁸⁶C	L	O	S	E
W			⁹⁴G	O					N

Across

1. top
8. in
33. day
41. down
57. no
63. run
69. from
81. on
86. open
94. stay

Down

1. small
3. fat
5. off
10. bottom
27. go
35. boy
39. slow
61. fast
70. close

¹S	O	U	R		⁶L	O	N	G
L		U		A				²⁰B
²¹O	P	E	N		²⁶D	A	²⁸D	A
W							O	C
	⁴²P	U	⁴⁴S	H			W	K
⁵¹Y			O		⁵⁶M	E	N	
E		⁶⁴U	P					⁷⁰T
⁷¹S	O	F	T		⁷⁶B	O	Y	A
			H					K
⁹¹N	E	W		⁹⁵S	Q	U	A	R	E

Across

1. sweet
6. short
21. close
26. mom
42. pull
56. women
64. down
71. hard
76. girl
91. old
95. round

Down

1. fast
6. lass
20. front
28. up
44. north
51. no
70. give

Crossword Puzzles—Using Synonyms and Antonyms

TEACHER: "Synonyms are words with the same or nearly the same meaning. Antonyms are words with opposite meanings. Solve the puzzle below using antonyms across and synonyms down.

¹F	A	²S	T	■	³G	O	O	⁵D
E	■	N	■	⁶W	O	N	■	⁷I N
E	■	O	■	■	■	■	■	N
L	■	⁸W	R	O	N	⁹G	■	¹⁰N O
■	■	S	■	■	■	U	■	E
■	■	¹¹T	O	P	■	N	■	R
■	■	O	■	■	■	■	■	■
■	¹²F	R	O	N	T	■	¹³C	■
¹⁴S	U	M	■	■	¹⁵F	L	A	T
■	R	■	¹⁶U	P	■	■	R	■

Across

Write an antonym for:
1. slow
3. bad
6. lost
7. out
8. right
10. yes
11. bottom
12. back
14. difference
15. round
16. down

Down

Write a synonym for:
1. touch
2. blizzard
3. leave
4. upon
5. evening meal
9. rifle
12. animal skin
13. automobile

Using Homonyms

PURPOSE: To expand word meanings.

PROCEDURE:
1. Prepare a sheet with a number of sentences with blanks to be filled.
2. Underneath the blank write two homonyms.
3. Pupils must read the sentences and write in the correct word to complete the meaning of the sentence.

TEACHER: "Homonyms are words that are pronounced the same but have different spellings and different meanings. Fill the blanks with the correct homonym."

1. We eat _____.
   (meat–meet)
2. I went to the movie to _____ my friend.
   (meat–meet)
3. The sum of one and one is _____.
   (to–too–two)
4. We went _____ visit the zoo.
   (to–too–two)
5. Her dress was _____.
   (blue–blew)
6. Sally _____ out her birthday candles.
   (blue–blew)
7. We walked down the dusty _____.
   (rode–road)
8. Jim _____ his bicycle to school.
   (rode–road)
9. The children answered roll call by saying, "_____."
   (here–hear)
10. The music was so loud we could not _____ her sing.
    (hear–here)

_____

TEACHER: "Fill the blanks with the correct homonym."

1. The _____ was very cold.
   (air, heir)
2. She was _____ to a large fortune.
   (air, heir)
3. At Christmas time we celebrate the _____ of Jesus.
   (birth, berth)
4. On the train, I like to sleep in the upper _____.
   (birth, berth)
5. My friend wants to be a _____.
   (none, nun)
6. The boy would share _____ of his candy.
   (none, nun)

7. The man worked in the _____ mill.
   (steel, steal)
8. The man was arrested trying to _____ a car.
   (steel, steal)
9. The chimney sweeper cleans the _____.
   (flew, flue)
10. The birds _____ south as the seasons changed.
    (flew, flue)

Crossword Puzzles Using Homonyms

TEACHER: "Homonyms are word that sound alike but are spelled differently and have different meanings. Work the puzzle using homonyms."

¹W	A	I	⁴S	T		⁷H	A	I	R
H			E		¹⁶H				
²¹O	H		²⁴A	T	E				
L		³³P		³⁶R	E	A	D		
E		A		E					⁵⁰N
		I							O
⁶¹M	A	N	E				⁶⁸P		T
A			⁷⁵T				A		
I			W		⁸⁷W	R	A	P	
D		⁹³T	O	O			E		

Across	Down
1. waste	1. hole
7. hare	4. see
21. owe	16. hear
24. eight	33. pane
36. reed	50. knot
61. main	61. made
87. rap	68. pair
93. to, two	75. to, too

¹T	²W	O		⁴S	U	N		⁷D
	O			E		¹⁰O		E
¹²N	O	T		E		¹⁶K	N	E	W
	D		²¹S			E		
		²³N	O		²⁵B			
	²⁶B		²⁷M	A	I	L		³¹S
³²H	E	³⁴R	E		R		³⁷A	T	E
	E			T		E		
⁴³R	O	D	E		⁴⁷H	⁴⁸O	L	E
					H		L	

Across

1. to, too
4. son
12. knot
16. new
23. know
27. male
32. hear
37. eight
43. road
47. whole

Down

2. would
4. sea
7. do
10. won
21. sum
25. berth
26. bee
31. steal
34. read
48. owe

					¹B	E		²T
³S	E	E	⁴N		L	.	⁵S	O
E			O		U		E	
A				⁶H	E	⁷R	E	
⁸M	E	E	⁹T	A		E		
		¹⁰A	I	R		A		
¹¹A	¹²I	L		E		¹³D	E	¹⁴W
	¹⁵N	E	¹⁶W					E
		¹⁷O	W	E				A
¹⁸P	A	I	N			¹⁹F	O	R

	Across		*Down*
1.	bee	1.	blew
3.	scene	2.	two
5.	sew	3.	seem
6.	hear	4.	know
8.	meat	5.	sea
10.	heir	6.	hair
11.	ale	7.	red
13.	do	9.	tail
15.	knew	12.	inn
17.	oh	14.	ware
18.	pane	16.	one
19.	far		

Find the Wrong Word

TEACHER: "The following sentences may *sound right*, but they should not look right to you. Each sentence contains one wrong word. Underline the wrong word. On the blank space, write the word that should have been used."

EXAMPLE: The opposite of wrong is *write.* __*right*__

1. He had to weight more than an hour for his dinner. _____
2. Smokey the Bare is the symbol for fire prevention. _____

3. The teacher asked Jane, "Will you please clothes the window?"
   _____

4. The movie was about a great heard of elephants. _____
5. Sugar is made from sugar cane and sugar beats. _____
6. Do you know witch came first—the chicken or the egg? _____
7. The whether man predicted showers. _____
8. Have you seen the new golf coarse? _____
9. The Texan said, "I'll take my stake medium rare!" _____
10. The club wanted to raze a thousand dollars. _____

Synonyms, Antonyms and Homonyms

TEACHER: "Stimulus words below are followed by three test words, each of which is a:

Synonym (S) same meaning
Antonym (A) opposite meaning
Homonym (H) same pronunciation, different spelling and meaning

On the space preceding each test word, write the one letter (S, A, H) which describes that word's relationship to the stimulus word. One line or series may contain the same category more than once."

SAMPLE: right: _S_ correct   _H_ write   _A_ wrong

1.	steal	___steel	___take	___give
2.	new	___antique	___knew	___recent
3.	waste	___squander	___waist	___conserve
4.	pale	___wan	___ruddy	___pail
5.	scent	___odor	___cent	___sent
6.	male	___female	___mail	___masculine
7.	soar	___rise	___sore	___plummet
8.	coarse	___crude	___refined	___course
9.	vain	___vane	___conceit	___vein
10.	alter	___altar	___change	___modify
11.	cite	___site	___location	___sight
12.	weak	___feeble	___week	___strong

Critical
Reading

If one closely examines "reading instruction," it becomes obvious that each unit of instruction deals with one or possibly several isolated reading skills. As a rule, we prefer to not think of instruction as being fragmented in this way. We are conditioned to view all instruction, even the teaching of specific skills, in the context of the ultimate goal of instruction—the production of critical readers. This view has some merit since it is true that no child can read a passage "critically" if he lacks any of the skills that are required for this task.

Critical reading is in essence a "language manipulating" process, and one must translate graphic signs into the language equivalents that the signs represent. To read critically, the reader must have facility with language that at least equals the demands of the material being read.

The school in its everyday operation invariably expects children to deal with larger units of work as illustrated by assignments to read stories, chapters in social science or science texts, or even trade books. This practice is followed even when students have not yet learned to efficiently "mine" smaller units such as sentences and paragraphs. Children who cannot easily determine the meaning of sentences and paragraphs can hardly be expected to cope with chapters and books.

The following exercises focus on smaller units of material for the teaching of critical reading. Children are asked to draw inferences, analyze fact or opinion statements, follow directions, detect malapropisms, and interpret proverbs and famous quotations. The difficulty level varies from first grade (riddles, opposites, etc.) to more difficult levels of *"interpretation."*

Stimulating Language Usage

PURPOSE: To stimulate critical reading and the manipulation of language through the use of riddles.

PROCEDURE: Present riddles orally while the children volunteer answers. (If children have the required skills, the material may be printed. Written answers may then be compared.)

1.   What goes up a hill without moving?   (a road)
2.   How are a cornfield and an elephant alike?   (they both have ears)
3.   How can you fix a loose tooth?   (with toothpaste)
4.   What goes down a hill without moving?   (a fence)
5.   How do you raise eggs in a garden?   (grow eggplants)
6.   Which are the best letters to eat?   (those in alphabet soup)
7.   What has a foot at each end and one in the middle?   (a yardstick)
8.   How is an elephant like a tree?   (both have a trunk)
9.   Name one dog that doesn't bark.   (a hotdog)
10.   What has eyes but can't see?   (a potato)

Riddles Based on Spelling of Words

1.   What is round at both ends and high in the middle?   (Ohio)
2.   Which river sees better than any other river? (the Mississippi—it has 4 i's)
3.   What part of a house needs a doctor? (the windows; they always have a pane)
4.   What is the only word you can make longer? (long)
5.   How can you change a pin into a tree? (add an *e* to the *pin*)
6.   What vowel has three letters? (*u—you; i—eye; a—aye*)
7.   What word can you make shorter by making it longer? (short)
8.   How can you change a bee into a vegetable? (add the letter *t—beet*)

Critical Listening/Reading: opposite meanings

PURPOSE: To provide practice in either listening or critical reading.

PROCEDURE (ORAL):   Teacher reads a sentence placing heavy stress on key or italicized word. The children provide the last word in each sentence. The word must have the opposite meaning of the stressed word.

READING EXERCISE: Prepare duplicated exercise sheets using sentences such as shown in the two samples below. Children complete sentences by writing a word which has a meaning opposite to that of the italicized word.

1.   The dog jumped *up* and _____.
2.   Santa wants to know if we've been *good* or _____.

3. Mother *found* the mittens I had _____.
4. When it rains we play *inside*, but when it is sunny we play _____.
5. When you finish your *work*, you may go out and _____.
6. During the day it is *light;* at night it is _____.
7. Ice is *cold;* boiling water is _____.
8. A rabbit runs very *fast* while a turtle is _____.
9. Sugar is *sweet;* a lemon is _____.
10. Sandpaper is *rough;* writing paper is _____.

---

1. Hang the *wet* clothes in the sun and they will _____.
2. She bought a *new* pair of skates and threw away the _____ ones.
3. It is *easy* to run downhill, but _____ to run uphill.
4. This pencil has a *dull* point; it is easier to write if it has a _____ point.
5. The road wound *up* the mountain, then _____ into the valley.
6. Airplanes fly *over* mountains while submarines can go _____ the water.
7. The *large* man was driving a very _____ car.
8. "You are *young* only once" said the _____ man.
9. The boys hoped to *win* the game, but unfortunately the team _____.
10. The guide flashed a *light* into the _____ cave.

Fact or Opinion Sentences

PURPOSE: To provide practice either in listening or critical reading to determine if sentences are statements of "fact" or of "opinion."

PROCEDURE (ORAL):   Pupils prepare "scratch-paper answer sheet" by writing a column of numbers 1 to 10, etc. Teacher gives the number of a sentence and reads the sentence. Pupils write O (opinion) or F (fact) for each sentence read.

READING EXERCISE: Prepare duplicated exercise using materials such as shown below.

DIRECTIONS: Read each sentence. If the sentence states a *fact*, write F in front of sentence. If the sentence states an *opinion*, write O.

_____ 1. We get white milk from brown cows.
_____ 2. Trees grow from seeds.
_____ 3. When you eat a sandwich, you should drink milk with it.
_____ 4. A duck has wings.
_____ 5. All words contain at least one vowel letter.
_____ 6. George Washington was our greatest President.
_____ 7. Boys are taller than girls.
_____ 8. Sunday is the best day of the week.

_____ 9. A building for farm animals is called a barn.
_____10. The fall season is very much like winter.

_____

_____ 1. Within ten years the U.S. will have a woman President.
_____ 2. The Pacific Ocean is the largest ocean in the world.
_____ 3. Large cities are not good places to live.
_____ 4. Eating carrots every day will help you to see better.
_____ 5. February is the shortest month of the year.
_____ 6. We will have astronauts on Mars in the near future.
_____ 7. An opinion may not be a fact.
_____ 8. The earth revolves around the sun.
_____ 9. Americans are the kindest people in the world.
_____10. The month of February may have either 28 or 29 days.

Sentence Meaning Exercise

PURPOSE: To apply critical reading skills.

PROCEDURE: For more detailed procedure see the preceding exercise. Children hear or read statements such as the numbered items shown below. They mark each statement as being either True (T) or False (F). This material does not teach-test word meanings, but it does call for: (a) careful attention to the text; (b) thinking while reading; (c) recalling and using essential facts.

TEACHER: Read each sentence. If the sentence is a true statement, place a T in the space before the number. If the sentence is false, write F.

_____ 1. A pound of wet sand is heavier than a pound of dry sand.
_____ 2. The word *level* spelled backwards is *level*.
_____ 3. Reno, Nevada, is west of Los Angeles.
_____ 4. A football is a game played by two teams.
_____ 5. Eight pints equal two gallons.
_____ 6. No person has ever been elected president of the United States four times.
_____ 7. Parallel lines can cross at only one point.
_____ 8. The word *Artic* in this sentence is misspelled.
_____ 9. "Four score and seven years" are more than one hundred years.
_____10. The Earth is larger than the Moon.

Following Directions

Sentence Tasks

PURPOSE: To provide practice in critical reading of sentences which provide directions for tasks.

PROCEDURE: Prepare a series of tasks similar to the illustration provided below.

TEACHER: "Read each sentence carefully and follow the directions."

1.   Circle all the words to which we could add *ing*.

car   go   walk   teacher   run

2.   Underline all the compound words.

anyone   desk   pocketbook   park

3.   Circle every odd number

5   12   24   7   11   18   9

4.   Underline every word that rhymes with *man*.

sun   can   sand   men   fan   ran

5.   Rewrite the following words so they make a sentence.

the   store   lost   the   got   in   child

_____

6.   Make each of the following words plural:

bird_____   bus_____   spy_____

dress_____   cow_____   fox_____

7.   Circle the words to which we could add the ending *s*.

ran   fan   can   car   is   this   teacher   girl

8.   Underline the words that contain one or more silent letters.

drum   comb   light   flag   knew

9.   Circle each word that rhymes with *me*.

see   toe   we   face   sea   key   they   sky   she

10.   Put the letter *t* in front of each word to make a new word.

__in   __old   __rain   __able   __all   __end

_____

1.   Cross out the word that doesn't belong.

orange   blue   sky   pink   yellow

2.   Circle the things that we can eat.

bread   sand   meat   purple   dress   cooky   brown

3.   Write the plural for each word.

man_____   dog_____

dress_____   fairy_____

4. Correct all misspelled words in the sentence below:

    we   all   wont   yoo   to   cume   ovir   to   cee   us

    ___ ___ ___   ___   ___ ___   ___   ___ ___ ___

5. Underline the words that rhyme with *cook*.

    stood   book   cork   took   good   book   look   hoop

6. Draw a line under all the numbers that come after *3*.

    7   2   4   1   6   5

7. Put the letter *s* in front of each word to make a new word.

    __and   __hop   __ink   __led   __it   __eat

8. Rewrite the following words so they make a sentence.

    and   went   Jack   up   hill   the   Jill

    _____.

9. Add the ending *ed* if it will make a word.

    went_____   want_____   do_____
    ask_____   tell_____   call_____

10. Underline all compound words.

    spelling   airplane   barnyard   soft   watchman
    typewriter   vacation   steamboat   dishpan   forget

    _____

1. Write the past tense of:

    run _____   sing _____   go _____

2. Underline the opposite of *high*

    tall   big   low   small

3. Circle the word if it is something you could do.

    hop   house   car   run   boat   read
    one   jump   play   each   sing   work

4. Circle every even number

    2   9   24   8   31   15   78

5. Write the plural for each word.

    mouse _____   tree _____   dish _____
    dress _____   tooth _____   fox _____

6. List these letters in alphabetical order:

    b   k   g   c   a   m   l

    ___ ___ ___ ___ ___ ___ ___

7. Write the contraction for:

    does not _____   can not _____   I will _____

8. Write a homonym for each word.

    eight _____   sail _____   meet _____
    steal _____   knight _____   wrap _____

9. Arrange each set of letters so they spell a word.

    erak _____   eno _____   reevy _____

10. Rewrite the following words so that they make a sentence.

    summer   our   for   it   almost   time   is   vacation

    _____ .

Sentence Directions

PURPOSE: To provide practice in critical reading of sentence-directions. Each sentence in the exercise relates to the material provided. The exercises are arranged in increasing difficulty. The first exercise deals with concepts left–right, top–bottom, and square–circle.

TEACHER: "Each of the printed directions relates to *Clock A* or *Clock B*. Read each sentence carefully and follow the directions given."

Clock A   *Clock B*

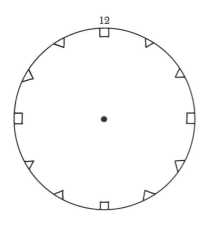
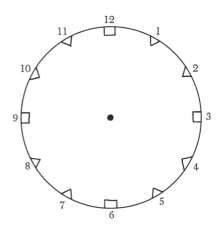

1. Put all the numbers around Clock A.
2. On Clock B, draw two hands to show 3 o'clock.
3. On Clock A, draw two hands to show 7 o'clock.

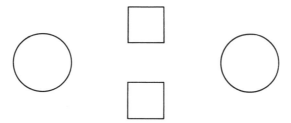

1. Color the circle on the right blue.
2. Put an X in the top square.
3. Color the circle on the left green.
4. Draw a line connecting the two circles.
5. Put a dot in the bottom square.

_____

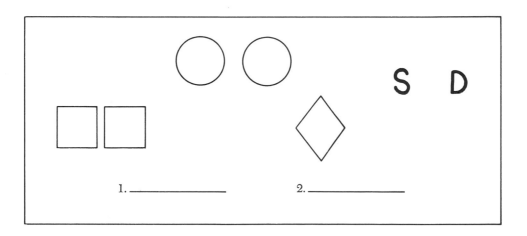

1. Draw a circle around the two circles.
2. Put an X in each square.
3. Draw a line from S to D.
4. Write a three letter word on line 1.
5. Put a dot in the diamond.
6. Write the opposite of *yes* on line 2.

_____

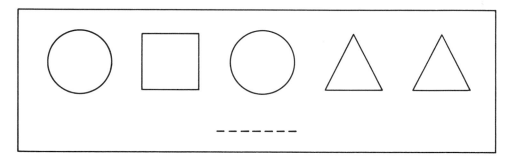

1. If the box contains 5 figures, write *yes* on the dotted line in the box.
2. If there are three circles in the box, put a dot in the first circle.
3. If there are three consecutive figures each of which is different from the other two, draw lines that connect these three figures.
4. If there are more circles than squares, put an X in the second triangle.
5. If there are as many triangles as circles, put a dot in the middle figure in the box.
6. If the last three figures in the box are triangles, put a dot in the square.

Key: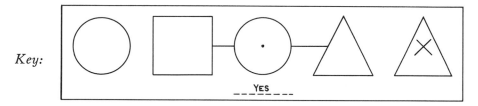

Other Activities for Following Directions

PROCEDURE: Duplicate an exercise page similar to the one shown below. In the illustration the pupils must be able to: (a) read the sentences; (b) know the meanings of *consonants*, *vowels*, *square*, *circle*, and *triangle*.

DIRECTIONS: How well can you follow written directions? Each sentence below asks you to study the box and then decide if you are to make a mark in the figures beneath the box.

1. If there is just one vowel in the box, put an X in the first circle.
2. If there are more consonants than vowels, put an X in the first square.
3. If the middle letter is a vowel, draw a line through the first triangle.

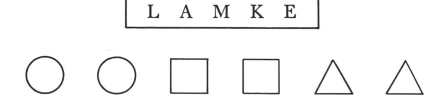

4. If there are two consonants together, connect the two triangles with a line.
5. If there are 5 different letters in the box, put an X in the second circle.
6. If the letter M follows a consonant, draw a circle in the second square.
7. If the second and third letters spell a word, draw a line under the two squares.

Key: ○   ⊗   ⊠   □   △–△

Context Clues

"Take away a letter"

PURPOSE: To provide practice in working with words and using context clues in sentence format.

DIRECTIONS: The first sentence in each series has one word underlined. You can take away a letter from this word and make a new word that will "fit" in the blank space of the next sentence. Continue this for each sentence.

1. Jack likes candy.
    His friend's name is _____.
    Jack _____ Andy are friends.
    They shared _____ apple.
    The boys always have _____ good time.

2. Ted paints a picture.
    Ted likes to _____.
    He cannot paint if he has a _____ in his finger.
    Did he get stuck with a _____?
    Yes, it went _____ his finger!

3. We saw a large boat on the lake.
    The cookies were made with _____ meal.
    I stayed _____ his house yesterday.
    We had _____ good time.

4. Rhode Island is a small state.
    A shopping center is sometimes called a _____.
    _____ of my friends like to go to the shopping center.
    I know a boy whose name is _____.
    He is _____ smart boy.

5. Our flag is sometimes called the Stars and <u>Stripes</u>.
   The top _____ on the flag is red.
   Each stripe is a narrow _____ of color.
   On our _____ we saw many flags displayed.
   A strong wind will sometimes _____ a flag.

1. Andy, and, an, a; 2. paint, pain, pin, in; 3. oat, at, a; 4. mall, all, Al, a; 5. stripe, strip, trip, rip.

Critical Reading: Paired Associates Context Clues

PURPOSE: To provide practice in using context clues.

PROCEDURE: Explain the concept of word pairs, "If I say bread, you would say _____." (butter) "If I say table, you would say _____." (chair)

Prepare sentences similar to those shown below. For oral language exercises, read the sentence, emphasizing the italicized word. One child, or the group in unison, supplies the proper word. For written exercises, children read the sentences and write the missing word.

1. Please pass the *salt* and _____.
2. Mother called, "Wear your *hat* and _____."
3. Before you eat, wash your *face* and _____.
4. A good breakfast is *bacon* and _____.
5. We had a snack of *cheese* and _____.
6. The teacher said, "Get out your *pencil* and _____."
7. The roads were covered with *snow* and _____
8. Dad ordered a cup of coffee with *cream* and _____.
9. He read the book from *beginning* to _____.
10. Wash your hands with *soap* and _____.

———————————

READING EXERCISE: In each of the following sentences write the word that "belongs" in the blank space.

1. We went to visit *Aunt* Jane and _____ Jack.
2. Father is a *man;* mother is a _____.
3. A *puppy* is a small dog; a _____ is a small cat.
4. My uncle has one *nephew* and one _____.
5. The senator has three children—two *daughters* and one _____.
6. Ted wanted a *bat* and _____ for his birthday.
7. We decided to order *spaghetti* and _____.
8. We need one more *cup* and _____ on the table.
9. I will need a *needle* and _____ to sew on the button.
10. They saw a *boy* and a _____ get on the bus.

———————————

1. In school, children learn to *read* and _____.
2. The little girl gave her Mother a *hug* and a _____.
3. This is a matter of *life* and _____.
4. He dug the hole with a *pick* and _____.
5. The girl fixed her hair with a *comb* and _____.
6. Dad hung the picture with a *hammer* and _____.
7. I cleaned the house from *top* to _____.
8. The child soon learned to put on his *shoes* and _____.
9. He always reads the *lost* and _____ column in the paper.
10. The man worked *day* and _____.

Profiting from Context and Phonic Clues

PURPOSE: To provide practice in using sentence context and letter clues in supplying a missing word in a sentence.

PROCEDURE:

1. Prepare a series of sentences in which a word is omitted but for which you provide the initial letter.
2. The child writes a word that keeps the sentence meaningful. (In many instances a number of different words may "fit" a particular blank. In the illustrations, words are shown. These should be omitted in preparing seat work.)

1. Jerry lost his c_____. (coat, cap, cup, car, cat, etc.)
2. Many enjoyed the b_____ very much. (book, ballgame, boxing, boys, boat, bear, baby)
3. His hobby is r_____. (reading, racing, riding, roping)
4. Beverly went over to Judy's to s_____. (swim, sing, swing, sew, socialize)
5. We all watched the m_____ on television. (man, monkey, movie, monster, meet, match, moon-walk, mobs.)
6. Monday was a very r_____ day. (rainy, rare, rosey, radiant, raw, rough)
7. The boys played with the t_____ they had received for Christmas. (toys, tops, trains, trailers, trucks)
8. The teacher dropped the book on my f_____. (foot, finger, fish, flower, feather, flag, folder)
9. "Oh my h_____ hurts," said Jane. (head, hand, hip, heel, heart)
10. Lucy asked, "Where are the g_____?" (gifts, girls, glasses, gowns, games)

_____

11. The large box contained many a_____. (apples, articles, animals, ants)

12.   My dog carried a b_____ into the back yard. (bone, box, bag, ball, bird)

13.   For her birthday she received many p_____. (presents, packages, pictures, pencils, pens, pennies, purses)

14.   As he read the paper he looked rather s_____. (sad, surprised, silly, stupid, stunned, startled, shocked)

15.   The diamond g_____ in the dark. (gleamed, glowed, glittered, glimmered)

16.   We watched as he r_____ down the ramp. (ran, raced, rolled, romped, rushed)

17.   Smoke b_____ from the tail of the jet plane. (blew, billowed, belched)

18.   Bobby's favorite game is b_____. (bingo, baseball, basketball, badminton, billiards)

19.   Many small c_____ lived on the farm. (children, chickens, cats, colts, calves)

20.   We saw a b_____ on the roof. (bird, bear, box, boat)

VARIATION: Move from sentences to brief sustained reading passages. In the first exercise below, each missing word must begin with the letter *t*. In the second exercise, no letter clue is provided. (Pupils may insert different words. Any combination is acceptable as long as the story makes sense.)

Gina and Tina are t_____. They like to play with their t_____. One of their favorite toys is a doll named Tammy. T_____ is a t_____ doll and the girls t_____ good care of her.

T_____ can walk and t_____. Gina and Tina often t_____ her to t_____ when they go to shop. Gina and Tina have a t_____ for Tammy's clothes.

The girls have a t_____ also. They t_____ Tammy for a ride on the t_____. Gina and T_____ enjoy T_____ so much it is a t_____ to watch them play with her.

(Key to words left out: twins, toys, Tammy, talking [tall], take, Tammy, talk, take, town, trunk, tricycle, tricycle, Tina, Tammy, thrill, [treat].)

Sally is my _____. We attend the same _____. Our homes are on the same _____.

Tomorrow is Sally's _____. Sally will have a _____. My _____ will take me to the party. Everyone will bring Sally a _____. We will play _____ at the party. Everyone will have _____. We hope the weather is _____.

(Key to words left out: friend, school, street, birthday, party, mother, present, games, fun, pretty.)

Drawing Inferences

PURPOSE: To provide practice in drawing inferences or conclusions which are not specifically stated in the material.

PROCEDURE: Exercises similar to the following may be duplicated for seat work, or the material may be placed on transparencies for use with an overhead projector.

1. "The moving van stopped in front of the empty house."
   (a)   The truck was probably empty.
   (b)   The truck was there to pick up furniture.
   (c)   The truck contained furniture of the people moving into the house.

2. "The airplane picked up speed as it came down the runway."
   The airplane . . .
   (a)   is landing at the airport.
   (b)   is taking off.
   (c)   is taxiing to the hangar.

3. "The taxicab made a U-turn on 12th Street."
   The driver . . .
   (a)   saw a man who wanted a cab.
   (b)   was practicing U-turns.
   (c)   thought a policeman was following him.

4. "Coming out of the barbershop, the man put his hand on his head and rushed back into the barbershop."
   The man . . .
   (a)   wanted to get a haircut.
   (b)   had forgotten to phone his wife.
   (c)   had left his hat in the barber shop.

5. "All day the wind made a whistling sound through the barren trees."
   It was probably a day . . .
   (a)   in early June.
   (b)   in the middle of December.
   (c)   near the 4th of July.

6. "Mother looked out the window and said, 'There will be no picnic today.'"
   Mother saw that . . .
   (a)   a truck was blocking the driveway.
   (b)   the neighbors were going fishing.
   (c)   it was raining very hard.

7. "The woman dashed excitedly to the fire alarm box."
   She wanted to . . .

(a) see where the fire was.
(b) report a fire.
(c) leave a note for the fireman.

Reading for Inference

PURPOSE: To provide practice in critical reading.

PROCEDURE: Prepare exercises on stencil to be duplicated so that each child may check the correct answer on the original sheet, or prepare exercises on transparencies for the overhead projector and let pupils read the exercise and write the correct answer on a separate sheet of paper.

EXAMPLES:

She shivered as she walked across the campus toward her class. The sun made patterns on the sidewalk as it defined the leafless trees. "Two more weeks," she thought. "Two more weeks until vacation, and then I'll see Tom." She turned up her collar before climbing the steps and entering the ivy-covered building.

1. What does this girl do?
    a. She works in a factory.
    b. She is a student.
    c. She is a housewife.
2. How old is this girl?
    a. Between 10 and 12.
    b. Between 18 and 21.
    c. Between 35 and 40.
3. Who is Tom?
    a. Her boyfriend.
    b. Her brother.
    c. Her son.
4. What is the weather like?
    a. Cold and overcast.
    b. Cold and sunny.
    c. Warm and sunny.

Fifteen dollars; only five more to go. Soon she will be able to get that cute little ball of fur that wags its tail at her every day. He looks so lonely sitting in the store window. If Jane can get a few more baby sitting jobs, she will be able to show him all the love a ten-year-old has to give.

1. What wagged its tail at Jane?
    a. cat; b. dog; c. monkey
2. Where did Jane see the "ball of fur"?
    a. her friend's house; b. grocery store; c. pet store
3. How much money does the pet cost?
    a. $20; b. $5; c. $15
4. Where is Jane getting the money?
    a. her mother; b. bank; c. earning it
5. How does Jane feel about pets?
    a. dislikes them; b. loves them; c. never thinks about them

---

Tomorrow is the big day. John has been practicing ever since school started. Now is his chance to show all his friends his special tricks. This is the time of year when spooky things are really popular. He doesn't even need to wear a costume to scare people. After the parade the older kids get to put on a show for the little ones. Gee! it will be great fun to see their faces turn white. It's a good thing it will be on the last day of the school week. They will have the weekend to recover from their fright.

1. What day of the week will something important take place?
   a. Saturday; b. Sunday; c. Friday
2. How long has John been practicing?
   a. about 2 weeks; b. about 2 months; c. about 2 hours
3. What kind of tricks will John do at the show?
   a. knife tricks; b. scary tricks; c. rope tricks
4. What holiday do you think it is?
   a. Halloween; b. Christmas; c. Easter
5. What children will see the show?
   a. college students; b. elementary children; c. high school children

---

Bob stared blankly out of the window as Mr. Jones repeated his directions. Bob saw all the rest of his friends begin to fill their papers as quickly as they could move their pencils. If only that late, late show last night hadn't been about the vampires. He certainly could have put his time to better use if he didn't enjoy horror movies so much. Multiplication of fractions was not the topic of the movie, so Bob may have a little trouble completing this morning's assignment.

1. Where was Bob?
   a. home; b. school; c. movie
2. What was he supposed to do?
   a. read a book; b. give a speech; c. take a test
3. Who was Mr. Jones?
   a. his friend; b. his teacher; c. his father
4. What kind of test did Bob have to take?
   a. reading; b. English; c. mathematics
5. When did Bob go to bed the night before?
   a. 2:00 A.M.; b. 8:00 P.M.; c. 10:00 P.M.

Slowly the battered green canoe cut its path through the murky water. Jim lowered his head when he felt trickles of water from the green overhanging branches go down the back of his neck. At the cave's outlet three turtles dived once again into the brown water from their perch upon several rotten logs. After clearing away the debris of sticks and bark, his strokes acquired a steady, even rhythm. Perhaps those canoe races at scout camp last summer were what gave him this confidence. Never had he seen these waters so high or the current so strong.

1. The season of the year suggested is
   a. fall; b. winter; c. summer
2. The weather has been
   a. rainy; b. hot; c. cool
3. Jim is
   a. an older man; b. a young man; c. a middle-aged man
4. Jim was paddling his canoe in
   a. a river; b. a small pool; c. an ocean

The loud and long wail broke the silence of the night. In the sky could be seen the telltale signs of orange streaks. Lights went on in the darkened homes around the block and windows were quickly raised by the sleepy residents. Barking dogs and shivering people soon lined the icy street to watch the long, sleek, red trucks whiz by with their sirens moaning the news. What had been a sleeping neighborhood was now a frantic beehive of commotion and anxiety.

1. What was the danger?
   a. flood; b. fire; c. tornado
2. What were the people watching along the street?
   a. an ambulance; b. police car; c. fire engines
3. What season of the year was it?
   a. spring; b. winter; c. fall
4. Where did the story take place?
   a. a city; b. a farm area; c. a small town
5. What time of day was it?
   a. noon; b. early morning; c. afternoon

Finding the Sentence That Doesn't Fit

PURPOSE: To provide practice in noting context clues and specifically finding a sentence in a paragraph that "does not fit."

PROCEDURE: Duplicate a page which contains several unrelated paragraphs (samples shown below). Each paragraph will contain a sentence that "does not fit." Children underline those sentences.

DIRECTIONS: Read each paragraph carefully and underline the sentence that does not fit, or which does not make sense in the paragraph.

1. Mother was baking a cake for Tommy's birthday. She sifted flour, added 2 eggs, and put it in the oven to bake. It seemed to take forever

for it to be done. At last the potatoes were ready. The frosting was chocolate with marshmallows.

2. Spot is a little brown and white dog. He is only six months old. A cat has nine lives. Spot loves to run and play. He plays tag with his tail and hide and seek with us. All day long he runs and plays in the sun. When he gets tired, he just plops down and goes to sleep.

3. I like to play baseball with my friends after school. Sometimes we play on Saturday. We wear white shirts and red baseball caps. Boots and mittens keep us warm. After we finish playing ball, we have Kool-Aid and cookies at my house. I wish we could play baseball every day.

4. Betty went fishing with her father. They left very early in the morning. Betty had made a picnic lunch. It was very good. Mother did the wash. After eating lunch they fell asleep and never did catch any fish.

5. The busy beaver is smart and works hard. He has very large, sharp teeth, and is able to cut down small trees with them. His webbed hind feet are for swimming. He can blow water out of his trunk. The beaver can build dams in streams.

Famous Sayings (scrambled)

PURPOSE: To provide practice in critical reading.

PROCEDURE: Prepare sheets of scrambled famous sayings. Let pupils write the sayings in their proper form.

EXAMPLE:

1. stitch in a time nine saves.
   A stitch in time saves nine._____

1. before leap look you.

   _____

2. bush a hand is bird two in the worth in the.

   _____

3. many cooks too spoil the broth.

   _____

4. invention is mother of necessity the.

   _____

5. runs still water deep.

   _____

6. stone gathers no a rolling moss.

_____

7. makes waste haste.

_____

8. nature law first self-preservation the is of.

_____

9. saved penny a is earned penny a.

_____

10. worm bird catches the early the.

_____

Detecting Malapropisms

PURPOSE: To teach critical reading, noting words that "do not fit."

PROCEDURE:

1. Explain that people sometimes confuse words. They use one word when they really meant to use another. The words confused are often similar in sound or spelling.
2. Develop a series of sentences each of which contains a malapropism or word that has a different meaning than the intended word.

TEACHER: "There is one word in each sentence that 'does not fit.' Underline this word. In the blank space following each sentence, write the word you think was intended."

1. May I have the vanilla folder?   _____
2. Anna was absent because she had the chicken-pops.   _____
3. At the museum we saw the Egyptian mommy.   _____
4. The word big is a cinnamon for large.   _____
5. Conversation experts fight forest fires.   _____
6. She was proud of her long blonde trestles.   _____
7. The government banned germ-welfare.   _____
8. They made many New Year's revolutions.   _____
9. John's father couched the baseball team.   _____
10. Some people use lemon with tea and some use sugar. I prefer the ladder.   _____

_____

1. Hurry and distinguish the fire before it spreads.   _____
2. We watched the cowboys riding bulls at the radio.   _____
3. The cantelopes ran across the field.   _____

4. The alphabet contains vowels and constants. _____
5. Firemen get water from a fire hydrogen. _____
6. The land along the river was very futile. _____
7. She chose the lasso of two evils. _____
8. "As you sow, so shall you also weep." _____
9. The garbage scowl chugged up the river. _____
10. In geometry we study squares angels and circles. _____

---

1. The thick window shade did not omit the sunlight. _____
2. The doctor gave me a subscription to be filled at the drugstore. _____
3. The police comprehended the criminal after a long chase. _____
4. I hope the catsup I spilled won't strain the rug. _____
5. Children should inspect their parents wishes. _____
6. That is a very good offer; you should except it. _____
7. My big brother gave his girlfriend a diamond, and now they are enraged. _____
8. She sprained the linament in her leg. _____
9. Her condition approved at the hospital. _____
10. Riding the alligator is much faster than climbing the steps. _____

The Analysis and Discussion of Smaller Units of Language

PURPOSE: To provide practice in critical reading skills.

PROCEDURE: Provide each student with a list of short "sayings," proverbs or "pearls of wisdom." Let pupils read the list and take turns discussing the meanings of the statements orally, or pupils may write the meanings on a separate sheet of paper.

Example:

1. It is easier to love mankind than it is to love your neighbor.
2. All mankind is of one author.
3. As face answereth face in water, so the heart of man speaketh to man.
4. Every man of learning eventually becomes his own teacher.
5. Don't give advice until you are called upon.
6. Many receive advice; only the wise profit by it.
7. It is sheer madness to live in order to be wealthy when you die.
8. The best answer for anger is silence.
9. Children need good models not critics.
10. Common sense is not so common.

1.   Neither the foolish nor the dead change their opinions.
2.   Discontent is often the first step toward progress.
3.   You can judge a man by his foes as well as by his friends.
4.   We forgive in proportion to how much we love.
5.   Never injure a friend, even in jest.
6.   An angry man opens his mouth and closes his mind.
7.   No man has ever become great by criticizing others.
8.   When you are on the side of the majority, it is time to reform.
9.   If a man does not keep pace with his companions, perhaps it is because he hears a different drummer.
10. Indecision breeds distrust.

---

1.   It is easy to believe what you have hoped for.
2.   Reading is to the mind what exercise is to the body.
3.   A good start is half the race.
4.   All people smile in the same language.
5.   You must have a good memory to be a successful liar.
6.   Mighty oaks from tiny acorns grow.
7.   All that glitters is not gold.
8.   Less than your best is failure.
9.   For success you need a backbone, a wishbone, and a funny bone.
10. The longest journey begins with one step.

Reading-
and-
Writing;
Dramatization

Integrating reading and writing activities is one of the best ways to help children understand how their language works. Instruction can ignore labels for parts of speech and other such rules, and children will still learn syntax by combining and expanding sentences and rewriting scrambled word orders.

Children will note the inherent logic of language usage when they arrange sentences into meaningful paragraphs. They can become aware of the precision that can be achieved with language when they attempt to write directions for simple activities such as playing Hop-Scotch, Tic Tac Toe, or how to get from school to the nearest hospital or fire station.

Learners discover that what they write actually becomes reading and that they can improve their reading ability by reading what they and their friends have written. Working with language is highly motivating and the reading–writing activities can focus on children's interests. Their interests can then lead to reading the more conventional materials that the school cherishes so highly.

Working with oral language leads to important insights relative to the power, flexibility, and precision of language. Children note that gaining precision with language is a long-term process, not something that is mastered with one exercise. However, they also note that they can start the process now! Learning to describe how a paper clip works is part of the continuum that eventually leads to explaining how a jet engine works or how to perform heart surgery.

Working with the Sentence Unit

PURPOSE: To provide practice in integrating reading and writing, specifically combining words into sentences, rearranging scrambled word order, combining sentences, and expanding sentences.

Word Storehouse

PROCEDURE: Print a number of words on oak tag or cardboard pieces and place them in a manila envelope (storehouse). A number of different store-houses may be prepared, some of which are general in nature; others may conform to a theme such as Writing a Letter, Halloween, Thanksgiving Day, Signs of Spring, etc. Children use the words in a storehouse to make sentences, or several sentences may be combined into a story.

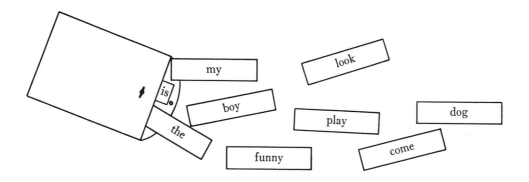

SENTENCES

1. *Look* at the *boy.*
2. The *dog* is *funny.*
3. *Come* out and *play* with me.

STORY

My dog is funny. I like to play with my dog.
My friends come over to my house and we all
play with my dog.

Scrambled Sentences

PROCEDURE: Write scrambled sentences on oak tag strips which can be in-serted in a Plymouth Chart. Children select one or more strips and write the words to make a sentence. Several sentences which tell a story may be used. Both sentence order and words within sentences may be scrambled.

Example:

Plymouth Chart

Sentence Garden
my coat see new
fun reading is
bicycle new I have a
red is an apple
dog a my collie is

Halloween

coming Halloween soon is

have might a party we

dress up fun it will be to

witch's mask have I a

Combining Sentences

PROCEDURE: Using material such as shown below, illustrate on the chalkboard how two or more sentences may be combined. Prepare exercises which children can do as seat work.

TEACHER: "Combine each series of sentences into one sentence."

1.   Nancy has a new coat.
       Her mother bought it for her.

       _____.

2.   John has a dog.
       It is a Collie.
       It is a friendly dog.

       _____.

3.   I have a bicycle.
       It is painted green and white.
       My brother gave it to me.

       _____.

4. Cindy is a dog.
    She is a Cocker Spaniel.
    Her hair is brown.

    _____.

5. Mary found a frog.
    It was little.
    The frog hopped and hopped.

    _____.

6. Fred has a toy.
    It is new.
    His mother gave it to him.
    It is an airplane.

    _____.

EXAMPLE OF RESPONSES

1. Nancy's mother bought her a new coat.
2. John has a friendly Collie dog.   (John's dog is a friendly Collie.)
3. My brother gave me a green and white bicycle.   (I have a green and
    white bicycle that my brother gave to me.)
4. Cindy is a brown Cocker Spaniel.
5. Mary found a little frog that hopped and hopped.
6. Fred's mother gave him a new toy airplane.   (Fred has a new toy
    airplane that his mother gave to him.)

Expanding Sentences

In the hands of a skilled teacher, this activity will probably result in as
much pupil growth "per time unit invested" as will any activity in the school
curriculum. One should not conclude that this type of experience relates
primarily to learning to write. The child learns much about his *language* and
the *melody* of language which he must incorporate into reading. The less
emphasis there is on grammatical labels, the more the child will learn about
the word patterns (syntax) that English sentences will accommodate.

PROCEDURE

1. Start with any kernel sentence.

    John has a dog.

    Point out that this does not tell us much about the dog and invite chil-
    dren to suggest one or more words that tells what kind of a dog John
    has.

    (Breed)   John has a *Boxer* dog.
               (In succession, deal with size, color, characteristics, etc.)

    (Size)   John has a *big*, Boxer dog.

    (Color)   John has a big, *brown*, Boxer dog.

(Characteristic)   John has a *friendly*, big, brown, Boxer dog.
(Who is John?)   John, my brother. . . .
John, my friend. . . .
John, the man who runs the newsstand. . . .

Sentences can "fit" any grade or academic level. Variations are unlimited since the activity may be oral, written, or a combination of both. Chalkboard work provides excellent opportunities to teach punctuation facts.

2. Demonstrate different word patterns for the same message.

My brother John has a big, brown, friendly, Boxer.
The big, friendly, brown, Boxer dog belongs to my brother, John.

Paragraphs and Stories

PURPOSE: To work with units larger than the sentence, providing practice in following directions, encouraging creative writing, and developing organization skills.

Read and Do

PROCEDURE:

1. Set up "read and do" stations around the classroom.
2. In each station place an activity with written directions.
3. Inform the pupils of the stations and encourage them to visit the stations as part of reading activity or language arts period, and "read and do" some of the activities.

Suggested activities for the "Read and Do" Stations

STATION I: Cards with pictures and directions.

I am a bee.
Write a story about me.

STATION II: Cards for "Stories about You."

> *Write the answers to these questions:*
> 1.   What is your name?
> 2.   Where do you live?
> 3.   When is your birthday?
> 4.   Who are your father and mother?
> 5.   Who are your friends?
> 6.   What are your favorite games?

STATION III: Cards with incomplete rhymes.

> Copy and complete this rhyme:
>   Yesterday at the fair,
>   Mary won a ribbon for her _____.

> Copy and complete this rhyme:
>   One day in spring,
>   We heard a bird _____
>   As we went out to play,
>   The little bird flew _____.

Match and Write

PROCEDURE: Prepare a number of story titles, each on a separate 3 × 5 card. Have the children select a title and write a brief story (usually under 50 words).

These stories written by children can be edited and typed on 3 × 5 cards omitting titles. The stories are added to the "bank" to be read by other children who then write a title. The suggested title and story can be fastened together with a paper clip and discussed with the reader-writer at some appropriate time.

Example:

Titles

1.   My Summer Vacation
2.   A Day at the Zoo
3.   My First Train Ride
4.   How I Learned to Swim
5.   My New Pet

Stories *(one to a card)*

1.   Last summer I went to Washington, D.C. on my vacation. I visited the White House, Arlington Cemetery, the Capital building and the

Washington Monument. I enjoyed this trip very much. I want to go there again soon and see the other interesting and historical sights.

2. Sunday we visited the zoo. There are many animals to see. We visited the lions and watched them feed the cubs. We stopped and watched the bears. The most exciting thing was feeding the seals. I enjoyed my visit to the zoo very much.

3. Mother and I went to visit my aunt last week. We went on the train. This was my first train ride. I sat next to the window and watched the cities and towns flash by as we rode through the countryside. We ate dinner on the train also. I like to ride the train. I hope we make another trip soon.

4. Swimming is my favorite sport. I learned to swim last summer at the Y.W.C.A. I enrolled in the summer swimming class. We met every day for an hour. The teacher taught us how to float first. We then learned to paddle with our hands. When we could use our arms and legs together we found we were swimming with little effort. It seemed hard at first, but soon I got used to it and that is how I learned to swim.

5. I have a new pet. It is a little black and white kitten. I let her live in the clothes bucket. Her name is Twinkle. I play with Twinkle every day. One day I will bring her to school and let you see my new pet.

Building a Logical Paragraph

PROCEDURE: Place five or more related facts on the chalkboard or on 3 × 5 cards. Pupils are to write a paragraph which includes all of the facts given.

TEACHER: "Write a paragraph that includes all of the facts given."

Washington Monument

located in Washington, D.C.	555 feet tall
completed in 1884	can go to top by steps
hollow inside	elevator trip is 70 seconds
contains elevator	took over 4 years to build
walls are 15 feet thick at bottom	contains 898 steps

Apollo 13

3 astronauts on board	destination moon
blasted off April 8, 1970	had to fly the "Lem"
power failure 200,000 miles from earth	very cold inside ship
many stages	national appeal for prayers for safe return
dangerous return trip	darkness inside ship
in space for 3 days	landed safely

Brazil

language spoken is Portuguese	gold and diamonds are found in Brazil
Amazon River is in Brazil	

coffee, bananas, and sugar grow there

coffee is the major export

capital city is Brasilia

largest nation in South America

industries are mining and cotton weaving

south central region has the best climate

The White House

In 1814 there was a fire and it was rebuilt

the address is 1600 Pennsylvania Avenue

the White House is located in Washington, D.C.

Jacqueline Kennedy supervised restoration of several rooms

it was rebuilt again in 1952

completed when John Adams was president

in 1817 it was painted white

home of the President of the United States

today it has 107 rooms and 31 bathrooms

approximately one million people visit it each year

Four "W" Stories

PROCEDURE: Use four paper bags or four manila envelopes. Label each container as follows: (1) Who (characters); (2) What (action); (3) When (time); (4) Where (place).

On separate cards write the names of *characters*, *types of action*, *places*, and *times* (time of day, season, etc). Put all items of a given type in a separate envelope. Pupils draw a card from each of the four envelopes and write a story using the items they drew as the basis for the story.

Example:

(1) *Who*	(2) *What*	(3) *When*	(4) *Where*
Betty	jump	evening	home
Bob and Billy	riding	in the summer	on the farm
Kittens	crying	one day	in a basket
Puppies	barking	at night	in the back yard

Four "W"'s drawn: Kittens, crying, one day, in a basket

Story:

> One day our cat had some kittens. We could hear them crying in the house. They lived in a basket by the back door. We all loved the kittens very much.

Four "W"'s drawn: Betty, jump, evening, home

Story:

> Betty is a girl. She likes to play. When Betty goes home in the evening she jumps rope.

Four "W"'s drawn: Bob and Billy, in the summer, on the farm, riding

Story:

> Bob and Billy are friends. In the summer they visit
> on the farm and ride the horses.

Writing Letters

PURPOSE: To provide practice in reading and writing letters.

PROCEDURE: 1. Using 5 × 8 cards, write a part of a friendly letter on each card (greeting, body, closing, and signature). 2. Let pupils each choose three cards, put them together to make a letter, and copy the letter on a sheet of paper in correct form. Let pupils read letters to the class.

Examples:

Card 1.	*Card 2.*	*Card 3.*
Dear Mary	I have a new coat. It is brown plaid. I want you to come over this weekend and see it. Let me know if you can come.	Your friend, Beverly

VARIATION: The number 2 card may include a sentence for the beginning of the body of the letter and the child is instructed to complete the body as he writes the letter.

PROCEDURE: On strips of paper, write instructions for types of letters to be written (letters may be friendly, thank you, business, or invitational). Let children pick a strip and write the type of letter called for.

Examples:

1. Write a letter to a friend in the hospital.
2. Write a letter to your aunt, thanking her for a gift.
3. Write a letter inviting your friend to a slumber party.
4. Write a letter to the state capital asking for materials to use in your class.
5. Write a letter to a friend telling him about a movie or a TV program.

Writing Descriptions

PURPOSE: To provide practice in observing and writing descriptions of familiar objects, reports, directions for playing games, and definitions of terms used in sports.

Describing One's Surroundings

PROCEDURE: Prepare a number of strips of paper with instructions for writing descriptions of various familiar items.

Example:

Write a description of:

1. Your classroom.
2. The person sitting to your right.
3. Your bicycle.
4. The neighborhood where you live.
5. Our school building.
6. Lunch time in the cafeteria.
7. School buses loading and leaving after school.
8. The playground during recess (or before school starts).

Writing Directions and Definitions

It is difficult to write concise descriptions for playing simple games, giving directions, or explaining terms from sports. Have children carry out the following writing tasks and read their descriptions to the class. Encourage the listener to ask questions which focus on omissions or confusing statements.

TEACHER: "Write the directions for the following:"

Playing Hop Scotch.
Playing Tic Tac Toe.
Playing Capture the Flag, Musical Chairs, Drop the Handkerchief, Red Rover, Stick Ball, Hide and Seek, or other games children play.
Finding a book in the library.
Going from the school to the fire station (bus station, park, or any nearby building in the neighborhood).
Walking from this classroom to the cafeteria (or library, gym, etc.).

TEACHER: "Write an explanation of any of the following sports terms."

Football	*Basketball*	*Tennis*
Safety	Traveling	Set
Illegal Procedure	Zone Defense	Love
Screen Pass	Pivot	Mixed Doubles
Clipping	Technical foul	Game
On-side Kick	Screen	Double Fault

PROCEDURE: Display a large picture-advertisement (toothpaste, dog food, clothing, soft drink, travel, etc.), but do not read any text which may be part of the ad. Have children make a list of "key words" which they think the manufacturer would want to see in the ad. Then have them write the material they think should accompany the advertisement.

Writing "Make-Believe" Stories

PURPOSE: To provide practice in story writing and to encourage creativity.

Story Starters

PROCEDURE: Make up a number of beginning sentences for make believe stories. Place these sentences on 5 × 8 cards. Keep the cards in a file box or a manila envelope. Have children choose a card and write a "make-believe" story.

Example:

1. Yesterday I passed an old, empty house. I heard. . . .
2. Last night the wind was howling through the trees and I. . . .
3. The door opened with a creaking sound and the bats flew out of the. . . .
4. I saw a strange sight as I looked in the toy store window. The toys were having a party. The drums were. . . .
5. Jim and I were exploring high among the rocks when we saw the nest with three birds in it. We got up close to look at the birds and then we heard this terrible noise above us. There was. . . .
6. It was very dark and Jack was frightened. He thought he saw something moving across the street. Then he heard someone say, "Hey buddy, come here a minute." Jack. . . .

Picture Stories

PROCEDURE:

1. Provide snapshots of individual pupils. Children then write a biography or a story about themselves and paste the photograph on the title page.
2. Provide snapshots of some school activities (book fair, Halloween costume party, parents' visitation, science fair). Children use snapshots to illustrate individually- or group-produced stories about the event depicted.
3. Gather "news" pictures which need not be related to the immediate school surroundings (famous athletes, space launch, pollution scene, television series, visit to community or area by a famous person, etc.). Children write stories using pictures to heighten interest.

Examples:

| *Pupils' Photo* | *School Activity Photo* |

This is Mary.

Our School Christmas Party

Picture Sequence

Trace a series of pictures which suggest
a story. Child composes the story, orally
or written.

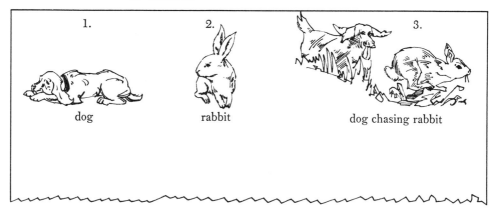

1.   dog   2.   rabbit   3.   dog chasing rabbit

Special Day Picture Stories

PROCEDURE: Collect pictures of activities that are characteristic of special
days or holidays and mount the pictures on pieces of cardboard. Let pupils
choose a picture and write a story about the activity and identify the holiday.

SUGGESTED PICTURES:

1. Santa Claus and his reindeers
2. Pilgrims—the first Thanksgiving
3. Hatchet and cherries
4. Bunny rabbit or colored eggs in basket
5. Pumpkins and witches

VARIATION: Stories with the pictures may be bound into a book of holiday stories for the class.

Picture-Stimuli (Projective Techniques)

PROCEDURE: Gather interesting pictures and paste each of them on a card or page. Children are instructed to "write a story about the picture." When the pictures are somewhat vague, the writer must "provide the context."

Write a story about this picture.

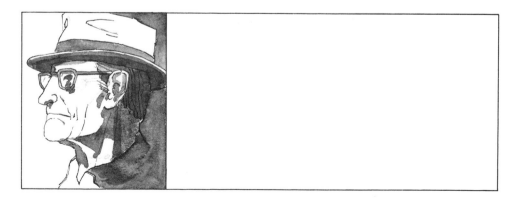

Finish the story: "In this picture the people are. . . .

Write a title for his picture. Then write the story.

When I look at this picture I think of . . .

Write a story about this picture.

Who is this? What is she thinking?

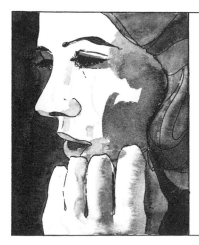

Writing a Book—Co-operative Class Project

PROCEDURE: Teacher and pupils gather pictures which relate to a particular day, event, or season of the year (Halloween, Lincoln's Birthday, Ground-hog Day, zoo animals, the Great Lakes, first men on the moon, Death Valley, etc.). The class and teacher develop a story which is written on the chalkboard. This group-developed story is then printed in a large class *Story Book* which is illustrated with the pictures which have been selected. These books are preserved and become part of the class library available to children at all times.

VARIATION: Instead of the class developing the story, pupils simply suggest *ideas* and *facts* which might go into the story. The teacher writes these on the board. No effort is made to organize or develop these ideas. When this activity is completed each child writes his own story and illustrates it with pictures he has found. (Other pictures will be available in the class *picture bank*. Pupils may select one or more of these pictures as governed by the ground rules that have been developed.) These books may then be circulated in the class. Some children may wish to *revise* their original stories.

Oral Language and Dramatization

PURPOSE: To provide practice in oral language usage and in dramatizing situations and stories.

Show and Tell (with a twist)

PROCEDURE:

1. A child describes a common object (pencil, paper clip, bobby pin, scissors, etc.).

    The *demonstrator* works from the assumption that no one in the group has ever seen or heard of the object and explains the object's design, material, function, etc. When the *demonstrator* is finished, the others in the class or group raise questions which were not explained.

    Illustration (child describing a 5¢ pencil): "This is a pencil. It is used for writing. The outside is made of wood which you see is painted yellow. Inside the wood is a long piece of lead. You cut away the wood and then the lead writes on paper."

    Questions: The pencil you showed is round. Are all pencils round? Are all pencils yellow? Are pencils always the same length as the one you showed? What's that metal strip near one end of the pencil? Explain the end that doesn't write (eraser), etc.

2. After several of these sessions the teacher can show a common object that has not been "discussed." Each pupil *writes out* the complete explanation of this object (*paper clip, pencil clip, paper bag*, etc.).

FURTHER TWIST: Divide children into groups of four or five. Each child in a group exchanges and reads the descriptions written by others in the group. Then, each child rewrites (edits) his original composition.

Memory Chain I

PROCEDURE: Teacher starts a story by providing the initial sentence.

Teacher: "John went to the store and bought *milk* and *bread*."
Volunteers are then called upon to say (in proper sequence) the items John purchased.
Child (1): "Milk and bread."
Teacher: "John bought *milk, bread* and *potatoes*."
Child (2): "Milk, bread and potatoes."
Teacher: "John bought *milk, bread, potatoes* and *rice*."
Child (3): (Continue to optimum number of items for group.)

VARIATIONS: When the game is terminated, *all* children write all items mentioned: (1) in order presented; (2) in any order (easier task). This game can also be played by two, three, four or more children in a group.

Memory Chain II

PURPOSE: Develops listening and oral language skills.

PROCEDURE: Prepare a series of cards, each of which contains a typed message. Each card is placed in a separate envelope. (Alternative approach: Record the messages on tape.) One child reads (or listens to tape). He then tells the second child the message. This child repeats the message to the third child, etc. (A cycle may include four or five children.) The last child in the cycle repeats the message to the group, each of whom compares this message with the original. The group then discusses the modifications that have occurred.

VARIATION: *When appropriate for group*, each member of the chain tells the next member the message and then immediately writes it down. Comparisons of written messages will help to point up where the changes occurred. (As a general rule, this activity need not focus on spelling of words.)

SAMPLE MESSAGES:

1. Last week on his birthday, John received a new bicycle. Last year, he was given a pair of skates.

2. Mrs. Charles Brown will visit our class tomorrow at 9:30 in the morning. She will tell us about national parks. She will show pictures of several parks including Yellowstone and the Grand Canyon.

3. A red fox was seen yesterday evening near the edge of Riverside Park. The fox was reported by Mrs. James Rogers who lives nearby. Mr. Williams, a game warden, said that sighting the fox in that area was quite unusual.

Attitudes or Emotions

PROCEDURE: Prepare a number of cards each containing one "attitude or emotion" word such as *sorrow*, *fear*, etc. Have the children draw (or choose) a word-card and, without using language, attempt to convey the meaning of the word through pantomime. (The children can work together on many presentations.)

Stimulus words:

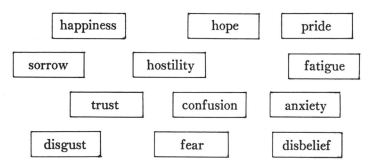

happiness		hope	pride
sorrow	hostility		fatigue
	trust	confusion	anxiety
disgust		fear	disbelief

Many Authors

PURPOSE: To develop creativity in oral language usage.

PROCEDURE: Teacher suggests "Let's work together and develop a story about a pet." One child begins the story and, at an appropriate point, a second child is invited to continue the story, etc.

ILLUSTRATION:

"Once there was a boy named Phil who loved all kinds of animals and living things. He liked turtles, and birds, and fish." (*Teacher calls on second pupil who continues.*)

"One day he saw a bird that could not fly. It was hopping along the ground and trying to hide in some bushes."

(*Third pupil*). "Phil decided to try to catch the bird and see if he could help it. He was very careful not to hurt the bird. . . ."

Follow up if appropriate to the group. Interrupt the story and ask each child to write his own version of how the story should proceed.

Book Reports

Too much emphasis on traditional book reports can turn children off and actually move them away from reading. While the following options emphasize oral language and dramatization, some can be adapted to written form.

1. Draw a picture or pictures to illustrate a high point of a story.
2. Prepare a sales pitch, "Why I'd recommend that you read _____" or, tell or write a summary up to climatic point in the story and let the listener (reader) hypothesize the outcome. This is also a method for "selling the book" to potential readers.
3. Act out a particular scene from a story or book.
4. Give an oral report to the teacher, a "story partner," small group or class.
5. When several children have read the same story, let them present a "panel review" or report.

Dramatization (acting out directions)

PROCEDURE:

1. Prepare a number of 3×5 cards each of which contains a one-sentence set of directions.
2. Volunteers select a card, read the directions silently, and perform the activity described.
3. Explain the task to the children: "Act it out without words." (Pantomime.)

SAMPLES:

1. Act like you are rowing a boat.
2. You are the pitcher in a baseball game.
3. Pretend you are sharpening a pencil.
4. You are the cheerleader at a basketball game.
5. All the seats are full when you get on the bus.
6. You are getting "a shot" in the doctor's office.
7. You put a coin in the milk machine—and it doesn't work.

PARTICIPATION:

Entire class.

Smaller group, or several groups working simultaneously.

Two teams competing: one child from Team A performs, members of Team B guess the activity. Alternate this procedure; the team with the fewest guesses wins.

Pairs of children (procedure same as teams).

Dramatization (an old myth)

PROCEDURE: Explain that you are going to tell a story in which there are three characters—

    a very poor woodcutter
    his wife
    a fish with magical powers

After you tell the story, the class will be divided up into "casts of three." Each group of three pupils will act out the story using their own words.

The story:

The woodcutter and his wife were very poor. One day the woodcutter went fishing. He caught a fine fish, and he thought how good it would taste for dinner.

Just then the fish spoke to him and said, "I have magical powers and if you will put me back in the water, I will grant the first three wishes that either you or your good wife ask."

The man decided that the three wishes would be better than eating the fish. So he put the fish back in the water. He hurried home and told his wife about the fish and what it had promised. The wife said he was very foolish to let the fish go.

The woodcutter was very hungry and pretty soon he said, "I wish we had a nice fish all prepared and ready to eat." Instantly, there appeared on the table a fine fish.

His wife saw this and shouted, "Look, you have wasted a wish—I wish that fish were on the end of your nose." Immediately the fish became attached to his nose and the poor woodcutter could not get it off. Finally, he said, "My, I wish I could get this fish off my nose." The fish was now back on the table.

FOLLOW UP:

After the children have acted out the story, change the game so that each child can write out the wishes he would make if he were granted three wishes. Discussion might follow as to which wishes are better than others.

Study

Skills

Good instruction should equip students to become more and more independent in searching out and acquiring knowledge. To be able to assume responsibility for their own intellectual growth, children must master a number of *study skills*.

Included among study skills would be *locating, evaluating, organizing, summarizing,* and *retaining* information. In addition to these skills, one must gradually become more economical and efficient in reading. This particular skill is often discussed under the headings of rate or flexibility. Good readers develop efficient reading habits. They do not read word-by-word; they combine words into thought units, and they can and do read different materials at different rates.

The need for efficient study skills increases as pupils advance through the grades. While they are needed in every curricular area, these skills may not be systematically taught in any of the curriculum areas simply because they are not part of the "content."

Our schools are often criticized for overrelying on textbooks. One of the reasons that the use of these materials is often quite inefficient, however, is because children have not learned how to "mine" a book. Many students do not profit from the reader's aids found in texts, such as the preface, index, table of contents, glossary, appendix, tables and illustrations, and the like. The materials that follow focus on a number of important study skills ranging from dictionary usage to improving rate of reading.

Working with Dictionary Skills

TEACHER: "Words in a dictionary are listed in alphabetical order. In the groups of words below, put a number in front of each word to show which would come first in the dictionary, which would come second, and which would come third."

Example: 3 cart   1 ant   2 ball

1.	—animal	—camel	—dog
2.	—rabbit	—mule	—tiger
3.	—goat	—snake	—deer
4.	—river	—boat	—jump
5.	—farm	—form	—fish
6.	—stove	—sink	—saw
7.	—pig	—pit	—pin
8.	—gate	—game	—coat

TEACHER: "Study the words in the box and write them in alphabetical order."

```
knot      knee      knob      knit

   knife      knock      knight      know
```

1._____   5._____
2._____   6._____
3._____   7._____
4._____   8._____

```
absent      abound      abroad      above

   about      absolute      able
```

1._____   5._____
2._____   6._____
3._____   7._____
4._____   8._____

Alphabetizing

PURPOSE: To provide practice in arranging a series of items in alphabetical order.

TEACHER: "In each of the following series, use the author's last name to list the items in alphabetical order. Place the number *1* in front of the item that would be first, the number *2* in front of the second item, etc."

_____Felton, Harold W., *Big Mose: Hero Fireman*
_____Deleeuw, Adele, *Paul Bunyan Finds a Wife*
_____Shapiro, Edna, *Windwagon Smith*
_____Caudill, Rebecca, *A Certain Small Shepherd*
_____Tarkington, Booth, *Penrod*

_____Clark, Leonard, *Flutes and Cymbols*
_____Dejong, Meindert, *Journey from Peppermint Street*
_____Nuefeld, John, *Edgar Allen*
_____Nyblom, Helena, *The Witch of the Woods*
_____Northrup, Mili, *The Watch Cat*

_____Buckley, Helen E., *The Little Pig in the Cupboard*
_____Shannon, Terry, and Payzant, Charles, *The Sea Searchers*
_____Hess, Lilo, *The Curious Raccoon*
_____Buck, Margaret W., *Where They Go in Winter*
_____Freeman, Mae, *The Book of Magnets*

_____Burch, Robert, *Queenie Peavy*
_____Blackburn, Jouce, *Martha Berry*
_____Bailey, Bernadine, *Picture Book of Georgia*
_____Burchard, Peter, *Bimby*
_____Berrill, Jacqueline, *Wonders of Animal Nurseries*

TEACHER: "Read the following authors and titles carefully and number them in alphabetical order. Remember, the author's last name is the key."

_____*The Little Girl and the Tiny Doll*, by Edward and Aingelda Ardizzone
_____*The Piemakers*, by Helen Cresswell
_____*The Battle of St. George Without*, by Janet McNeill
_____*The Foolish Bird*, by Henri Maik
_____*The Longest Name on the Block*, by Jane Yolen
_____*Pass to Win: Pro Football Greats*, by George Sullivan
_____*The Snow Firing*, by Joyce Gard
_____*Tall Sails to Jamestown*, by Eugenia Stone
_____*The High King*, by Lloyd Alexander

TEACHER: "In each series below, number the words in the order in which you would find them in the dictionary."

Sample:

_4_ gouge	____placate	____mansion	____realist
_1_ fabulous	____piston	____needle	____scribe
_3_ gossip	____pitiful	____pedestal	____tension
_7_ haggard	____place	____lava	____tentacle
_6_ habitat	____pitch	____organic	____union
_2_ faculty	____plane	____quill	____wave
_5_ governor	____pivot	____jaguar	____vacuum

____scandal	____observe	____gong	____tempt
____sandal	____oblong	____gone	____teammate
____sanitary	____oasis	____gorge	____tease
____scale	____oath	____gopher	____tendency
____sacred	____object	____good	____temperance
____satchel	____obstacle	____goober	____technique
____saint	____obey	____gondola	____telescope

Estimating Location of Words

PURPOSE: To facilitate use of a dictionary without tabs. To provide practice in entering the dictionary near the point where the desired word is located.

PROCEDURE: Discuss orally how the dictionary can be divided roughly into halves, A–M and N–Z, and into four sections, A–E, F–M, N–S, and T–Z. Pronounce a series of words one at a time and have the children open their dictionaries as close as possible to the stimulus word.

Examples: chair (section 1)   tin (section 4)
doorstep (section 1)   gate (section 2)
record (section 3)   zoo (section 4)
neighbor (section 2)   queen (section 3)

Using procedure outlined above, discuss dividing the dictionary into three parts: A–H (front), I–R (middle), S–Z (back). Provide duplicated list of stimulus words. Following each word, have the children write either *front*, *middle*, or *back* to indicate the approximate location of the word.

Example: fan   front   tiger   back

1. water _____	5. table _____	9. lamp _____
2. chair _____	6. monkey_____	10. basket_____
3. violin _____	7. kitten _____	11. gong _____
4. umbrella_____	8. apple _____	12. scale _____

PROCEDURE: Secure four boxes marked as shown below. Place a number of *word-cards* in each box. Difficulty is controlled by the number of words used;

words can be changed frequently. Have a child select a box and either write the words or arrange the cards in alphabetical order.

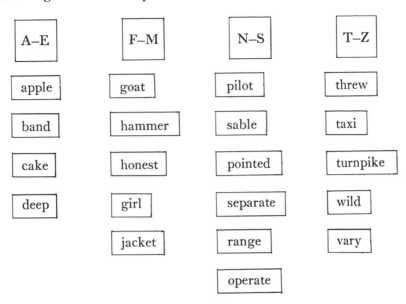

A–E	F–M	N–S	T–Z
apple	goat	pilot	threw
band	hammer	sable	taxi
cake	honest	pointed	turnpike
deep	girl	separate	wild
	jacket	range	vary
		operate	

Use of Guide Words

TEACHER: "The top of each page in the dictionary contains two "guide words." The word at the left of the page is the first word on the page, and the word on the right is the last word on the page."

Example: row   ruby

Circle the words below which you *would not* find on a page if the guide words are:

row	*ruby*
rubber	royal
run	rub
ruffle	rudder
row	rube

Circle the words not on page if guide words are:

sidewise	*signet*
silent	siding
siesta	sight
sign	signature
signal	silk

Underline the words that *would* appear on the page if the guide words were:

>   *profess*   *programming*
>   progressive   program
>   profess   prolific
>   profile   prologue
>   profit   profound
>   profession

Using the Dictionary for Word Meanings

PROCEDURE: Duplicate a page of sentences each of which contains one under-lined word. Beneath each sentence, have the children write as many synonyms as they can for the underlined word. Encourage use of the dictionary.

1. That house has been <u>vacant</u> for many years.

    _____

2. The mean queen had no <u>affection</u> for Snow White.

    _____

3. The explorers were looking for someone to <u>guide</u> them up the mountain.

    _____

4. The child was very <u>timid</u>.

    _____

5. The teacher was <u>upset</u> with the class.

    _____

6. Grandfather read them a very <u>exciting</u> story.

    _____

7. They were <u>happy</u> to hear the good news.

    _____

8. It was a very <u>generous</u> offer.

    _____

9. The girls kept their room very <u>neat</u>.

    _____

10. The law does not <u>permit</u> parking here.

    _____

Dictionary Maze

PROCEDURE: Set up a number of stations or areas in the classroom for study-ing dictionary skills.

Examples: 1.   List of words to alphabetize
              a.   first letters the same

  b. first two letters the same
  c. first three letters the same
  d. all initial letters different
2. List of book titles to alphabetize.
3. List of author's names to alphabetize.
4. Key word or guide word exercise. (Write the guide words on page where listed word is found.)
5. Underlined words in sentences to be substituted while keeping meaning of sentence the same.

Provide answer cards for pupils to check their work at each station. Let children work their way through the dictionary maze at their own rate of ability. Children may be allowed to work through the maze until they are able to complete each station activity correctly.

How to "Mine" a Book

PURPOSE: To provide experiences which lead children to a better understanding of how to use the various helps provided in most textbooks. (Examples: table of contents, index, glossary, etc.)

PROCEDURE:

1. Select any textbook (social studies, science, math).
2. Write a number of question-tasks, each of which will lead the learner to use one of the "aids to earning" found in the book.
3. A duplicated work sheet may be used with the class as a whole, then with small groups and individual pupils for review.

TEACHER: "Use your textbook to answer these questions."

1. The index begins on page _____ and ends on page _____.
2. List three types of information found in the appendix:

   _____   _____   _____

3. What key word do we look under if we wish information on Bonneville? _____ Grand Coulee and Hoover dams? _____
4. What page contains the populations and capitals of each state? _____
5. What page of your book has a picture of a *blockhouse* (use the index)? _____
6. Under the heading *Civil War*, you are told to see another heading. What is it? _____
7. How many subtopics are listed under the entry *Great Ideas?* _____
8. Are each of these listed somewhere else in the index? _____
9. Pages 482–492 are called an *atlas*. Study these pages; then write a definition of the term *atlas*.

10. Where do you find the definition of erosion? _____

11. On what page do you find data telling you which state has the largest and which the smallest area? _____

12. On what page will you find a picture showing erosion? _____

13. What is the pronunciation of *Sault St. Marie?* _____

14. Does your book contain a diagram showing how plywood is made? _____

15. Page _____ contains a list of all of the maps found in the book.

Using the Encyclopedia

PURPOSE: To provide an understanding of the encyclopedia as a resource tool and to provide practice in its efficient use.

PROCEDURE:

1. Duplicate a drawing that represents the various volumes in an encyclopedia set. (Show *volume number* and alphabetical coverage.)

2. Present questions orally which ask the student to identify the volume that would contain data on certain topics. (Discussion will focus on the importance of selecting the proper heading or topic.)

3. Prepare duplicated exercise similar to those shown in the illustration below.

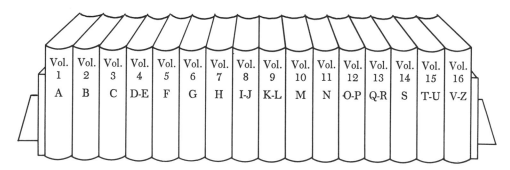

Using the above drawing, in which volume(s) would you likely find the most information about:

1. Soft coal production in Illinois: _____.
2. The Grand Canyon National Park: _____.
3. The population and area of Labrador: _____.
4. Birthplace of Andrew Jackson: _____.
5. Poisonous snakes found in United States: _____.
6. Occupation and nationality of Jan Sibelious: _____.
7. Burial place of U. S. Grant: _____
8. Site of Olympic games in 1904 and 1924: _____.

9. Known sources of Helium: _____.
10. City in which University of Idaho is located: _____.

"Private Eye"—Gets the Facts!

PROCEDURE:

1. Prepare statement sheets with certain facts left blank. The private eye searches through an encyclopedia to find the answers.
2. Cross referencing can be included by asking for a side point on a main reference.
3. The private eye writes his answers.
4. This exercise can be used with a large or small group.

Private Eye Exercise on George Washington

1. George Washington was born in the year _____.
2. His mother's name was _____.
3. In his early life Washington was a _____ and surveyed much land.
4. During the French and Indian War he served with General _____.
5. At the time of the American Revolution, Washington was asked to be the _____ of the colonial army.
6. After the war he was asked to be _____ of his country.
7. He died in _____.

Cross References:

1. His mother lived many years in _____, Virginia, where she is buried.
2. General Braddock was from _____.
3. The architect who designed the city of Washington, D.C., was _____.

Private Eye Exercise on Martin Luther King, Jr.*

1. Martin Luther King was the father of the _____ civil rights movement in the United States.
2. He won the _____ peace prize in _____.
3. King lived in _____, Georgia.
4. His first civil rights demonstration took place in _____, Alabama.
5. King was assassinated _____ in Memphis, Tennessee.
6. King was president of the S_____ C_____ L_____ C_____.
7. King's non-violent march on Washington, D.C. occurred _____.
8. King is remembered for his work with voter _____ and civil rights _____.

* Exercise based on 1968 and 1969 Yearbook of Compton's Encyclopedia.

Private Eye Exercises on United Nations

1. The President of the United States at the time of the organization of the United Nations was _____.
2. The United Nations building is located in _____.
3. The "Big Four Nations" that met to draw up plans for this organization were _____, _____, _____, and _____.
4. The supreme goal of the United Nations is to _____.
5. There are six basic organs of the United Nations:
   a.
   b.
   c.
   d.
   e.
   f.
6. The first secretary general of the United Nations was _____.
7. The present secretary general is _____.

One-a-Day

PROCEDURE:

1. Prepare a number of 3 × 5 cards each containing a fact question which is to be answered using the encyclopedia.
2. Each child has a lined sheet of paper which is labeled, "One-a-Day Sheet."
3. Children read as many of the question cards as they wish and select *one* they wish to answer. The child copies the question and his answer on his *one-a-day sheet.*

VARIATIONS:

1. Children can occasionally "exchange" their one-a-day sheet as a further reading exercise.
2. Once a week, or every two weeks, pupils select a card and write a *story* about the topic involved in the question.

Sample questions:

What is a mongoose? Is it helpful to man?	Where are the most productive diamond mines? Can you determine who owns them?
What is The Baseball Hall of Fame? Where is it located?	Who was the second man to walk on the moon?

Identify Susan B. Anthony	Who invented the game of basket-ball? In what year was the game invented? Where was basketball first played?
Compare the size of Alaska with that of the continental U.S.	
What poisonous snakes are found in the U.S.?	How long has man known about the circulation of blood?
Which are the three largest dams in the U.S.?	

Using Maps

Can You Locate the Various States and Major Cities on a Map of the U.S.?

TEACHER: "Using the map above, answer these questions:"

1. What western state is identified by the letter *A?* _____
2. What Atlantic seaboard state is represented by the letter *J?* _____
3. What is the name of the southern state marked *L?* _____
4. The midwestern state *F* is *Iowa.* Starting to the north and moving clockwise, write the name of each state which borders on Iowa.

    _____ , _____ , _____ , _____ , _____

5. Name the Southwestern state marked *D*. _____
6. The state marked *G* is the state of _____.
7. The letter *K* (extreme north-east) is in the state of _____.
8. Two thousand miles to the west, *C* is the state of _____.
9. The largest state shown contains no letter or number; it is the state of _____.

Identifying Cities

10. The number *2* represents the large industrial city of _____ located in the state of _____.
11. The Midwestern city (number *4*) is _____.
12. The number *8* represents "the mile high city" of _____.
13. The large eastern city (number *3*) contains many historical sites of the colonial and Revolutionary War periods. It is _____.
14. On the west coast, number *10* is the city of _____ and number *11* is _____.
15. In the southeast, number *1* is the city of _____.

Land routes, and bodies of water

16. Draw a line from Springfield, Illinois, to Oklahoma City, Oklahoma.
17. Place the abbreviation *L. Sup.* in the area representing *Lake Superior*.
18. In the appropriate places, write in *Gulf of Mexico, Atlantic Ocean,* and *Pacific Ocean*.
19. Draw a line straight from Milwaukee to Seattle.
20. What states does your line pass through? _____, _____, _____, _____, _____
21. Draw a dotted line from Boston to Pittsburgh.

TEACHER: "Use the above map to answer all problems below. In some cases you are to write on the map, in others fill in the blank spaces in the problem. All numbers on the map represent large or important cities."

1. Write *Iowa* in the proper space on the map.
2. Draw a line from Miami, Florida, to St. Louis, Missouri.
3. Number *2* on the map represents the location of the city of

   _____.

4. Write the abbreviation Penn. for Pennsylvania in that state on the map.
5. Write *N.D.* and *S.D.* in the states of North Dakota and South Dakota.
6. Write in the abbreviations of three states which border on the Mississippi River. _____, _____, _____
7. The state directly south of the state containing the number *5*, is the state of _____.
8. The state having the longest common border with California is the state of _____. (Write it on the map.)
9. Oklahoma City is number _____.
10. Number *13* on the west coast locates the city of _____.
11. Indianapolis is number _____.
12. Pittsburgh is number _____; Philadelphia is number _____.
13. Cleveland is represented by the number _____.
14. The number _____ represents the city of Milwaukee.
15. Salt Lake City is represented by the number _____ and is located in the state of _____.

16. Dallas and Fort Worth are neighboring cities represented by the numbers _____ and _____.
17. Seattle is represented by the number _____.
18. The city represented by the number *10* is the city of _____.
19. Draw a line from Seattle to Indianapolis so that it passes through Salt Lake City and Denver.
20. Draw a straight line from Dallas to Philadelphia.

Map Reading

Maps often contain guides for finding places or cities. Example *A* below tells us how to locate the city of Detroit. Example *B* locates Austin, Texas.

Example A: Detroit, Michigan, is found by drawing a line down from *17* and a line over from *F*. The place where the two lines meet is the location of Detroit.

Example B: Lines drawn from *10* and over from *L* locate the capitol city of Texas which is _____.

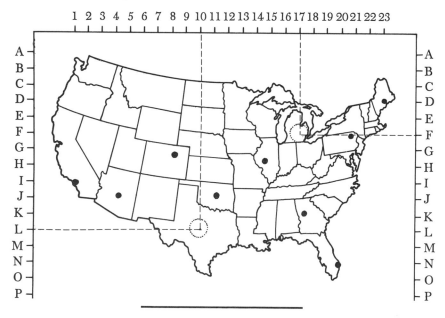

1 2 3 4 5 6 7 8 9 10 11 12 13 14 15 16 17 18 19 20 21 22 23

A B C D E F G H I J K L M N O P

TEACHER: "The problems below provide clues which will guide you to the location of certain cities. You are to name these cities. Complete all the problems you can without using a map. Then use a map of the U.S. if needed. (You need not draw lines on the map; use imaginary lines.)"

1. H–15   Capital of midwestern state; Lincoln buried there. _____
2. I–1   Not state capital, but the largest city in southern California. _____
3. J–11   Capital of southwestern state (Will Rogers country). _____

4. D–23 Capital of state located in northeast corner of U.S. _____
5. K–17 Capital and largest industrial city of this southeastern state.
_____
6. C–7   Straight lines drawn from these points would intersect in the state of _____.
7. F–21 Large city in eastern Pennsylvania (not capital). _____
8. J–4   Capital of southwestern state. _____
9. N–20 Atlantic coastal city. _____
10. G–8 State capital of the "mile high city." _____

Developing Flexible Reading Habits

Rate

PURPOSE: To provide intermediate-level students with insights into their reading habits; specifically to provide practice in "phrasing materials" in order to increase both rate of reading and comprehension of material.

PROCEDURE: Discuss the fact that as students move upward through the grades they are expected to do more and more reading. Therefore, they must develop more efficient reading skills. Place the following on the chalkboard and discuss.

Good Readers:

1. Do not read word-by-word.
2. Combine words into phrases.
3. The phrases are thought–units.
4. Read different materials at different rates.
5. Can read some materials rapidly; and they know when they should and should not read rapidly.

Word-by-Word Reading: A Bad Habit

Word-by-word reading is not efficient and causes one to be a very slow reader. It may also hinder the reader from getting the meaning of a passage. Each word and its relationship to other words must be kept in mind until the entire sentence is finished. For example, concentrate on each word separately in the following sentence:

The/good/reader/notes/very/quickly/those/situations/in/which/ he/may/read/rapidly,/and/he/has/developed/the/ability/to/read/ rapidly/when/this/procedure/is/justified.

Assume that a child reads all the time the way you read this sentence. The teacher should suggest that he read the passage again saying, "Read it like you would say it," or "Read it with expression." When you read with expression you group words into logical thought units and read phrases as single units.
Read the same sentence again. It is arranged in phrases.

The good reader notes very quickly those situations in which he may read rapidly, and he has developed the ability to read rapidly when this procedure is justified.

Test on Phrase Reading

The material below consists of phrases which gradually increase in length. Read down the columns. Try to read each phrase as one unit. Can you read the longer phrases as one unit?

can be	go now	try one
is a job	to a man	gave help
see it now	be so kind	one for all
fire at will	just so long	hear the bell
generally fair	will come soon	is well to take
change the parts	around the earth	became the rivals
difficult to trace	during this period	measured accurately
men worked for years	accurate observation	heard a lively debate

Practice Material: Medium Length, Unrelated Phrases.

Read down each column as rapidly as you can. Treat each line or phrase as one thought unit.

pet the dog	went to see	for instance
that is all	a way out	is very busy
saves times	adding to it	out of step
want to go	to the lake	clean it up
pointed out	not too easy	in the attic
lay it down	a big help	two or three
to the lake	did not go	at the farm
on the paper	read a story	to the house
eat some cake	on the slide	did not fall
in the shade	the big horse	word groups

Phrase Reading: Continued Text

Read down the columns as rapidly as you can. Read them several times and try to improve your rate.

Many students
feel that they
do not read
as effectively
as they should.
These students
are probably
correct.
      You can be
a better reader
by improving
your present
reading habits.
One important
reading skill
is *phrasing*.
Phrasing means
saying words
in groups.
In learning
to read
you probably
read each word
separately.
This is called
word-by-word
reading.

You should not
be reading
this way now.
When one reads
word-by-word
he reads slowly.
In addition
the meaning
of sentences
and paragraphs
is often lost
because words
are not combined
into logical
thought–units.
      This material
is arranged
in phrases.
Each line
should be read
as "one-unit."
These lines
of print
are no longer
than some
single words.
You can read

longer words
as one unit.
For instance,
    Mississippi
    thunderstorm
    comprehension
    association
    combination.
      With practice
you can also
learn to read
several words
just as easily
as you read
longer words.
You simply
combine words
into single
thought-units.
      This material
is provided
for practice
in reading phrases.
When you read
other material
you can do
your own phrasing.

Your Phrasing Pattern

In the following sentence the lines represent one way that the material could be phrased.

> *Today   one will find   very few positions   of responsibility   in business   or industry   which   do not call for   extensive reading.*

You can discover the "pattern of phrasing" that you use when reading. The material in the box below is taken from *The Declaration of Independence.* Read it through once. Then underline the words and groups of words which you "read as units." Doing this task may provide insight for answering these questions.

1. "Do you tend to read word-by-word?"
2. If you read in phrases, "Do you vary the length of the phrase?"
     "Do you read in 'logical thought units'?"

We hold these truths to be self-evident, that all men are created equal, that they are endowed by their Creator with certain unalienable Rights, that among these are Life, Liberty and the pursuit of Happiness. That to secure these rights, Governments are instituted among Men, deriving their just powers from the consent of the governed. That whenever any Form of Government becomes destructive of these ends, it is the Right of the People to alter or to abolish it, and to institute new Government, laying its foundation on such principles and organizing its powers in such form, as to them shall seem most likely to effect their Safety and Happiness.

(See page 108 to compare your phrasing with another model.)

More About Reading

This exercise
also provides
some material
which is phrased
in small units.
As you read,
your eyes move
fairly rapidly
down the page.
This is similar
to reading
a newspaper.
　　This material
is written
in short phrases
so that you
can practice
seeing words
in thought-units.
This helps you
read faster.
However,
remember also
that reading
in phrases
or thought-units
helps the reader
get the meaning.

When one reads
word-by-word
he must select
groups of words
that make sense.
　　Good readers
have developed
the ability
to read
some materials
more rapidly
than others.
More important
they also know
when they should
slow down.
　　There are many
reading skills
that combine
to produce
efficient readers.
These skills
also influence
how rapidly
one can read.
For example,
good readers
have a large

sight vocabulary.
(Words which one
does not need
to study
or "sound out.")
Efficient readers
know the meanings
of many words,
as well as
different meanings
for the same word.
They read widely—
which develops
"background."
This helps them
understand
more of what
they read.
Good readers
profit from
punctuation marks,
they read with
good expression.
But above all
they like to read.
One might say
"Good readers
are avid readers."

Declaration of Independence

. . . —We hold
these truths
to be self-evident,
that all men
are created equal,
that they are endowed
by their Creator
with certain
unalienable Rights,
that among these
are Life,
Liberty
and the pursuit
of Happiness.—
That to secure
these rights,
Governments
are instituted
among Men,
deriving
their just powers
from the consent
of the governed,—
That whenever
any Form
of Government
becomes destructive
of these ends,
it is the Right
of the People
to alter
or to abolish it,
and to institute
new Government,
laying its foundation

on such principles
and organizing
its powers
in such form,
as to them
shall seem
most likely
to effect
their Safety
and Happiness.
Prudence, indeed,
will dictate
that Governments
long established
should not
be changed
for light
and transient causes;
and accordingly
all experience
hath shewn
that mankind
are more disposed
to suffer,
while evils are sufferable,
than to right themselves
by abolishing
the forms to which
they are accustomed.
But when
a long train
of abuses
and usurpations, . . .
evinces a design
to reduce them
under absolute

Despotism,
it is their right,
it is their duty,
to throw off
such Government,
and to provide
new Guards
for their future
security.— . . .
WE, THEREFORE,
the Representatives
of the UNITED STATES
OF AMERICA,
in General Congress,
Assembled, . . .
do, in the Name,
and by Authority
of the good People
of these Colonies,
solemnly publish
and declare,
That these
United Colonies are,
and of Right ought
to be FREE AND
INDEPENDENT STATES, . . .
—And for the support
of this Declaration,
with a firm reliance
on the protection
of divine Providence,
we mutually pledge
to each other
our Lives,
our Fortunes
and our sacred Honor.

Teachers' Declaration of Independence

In conclusion—
we, teachers of reading
who, having noted
that many children
do not perceive
learning to read
as a joyful
happy experience,
—and furthermore
on occasion
having noted
that *teaching* reading
is not as rewarding
as we know
it should be—
we do now
solemnly swear,
(or where swearing
is frowned upon
or prohibited by law),
do solemnly affirm
that henceforth
we will improve
classroom vibrations
by helping children
to see that reading
is a language process.
Schools are instituted
in all societies
without the consent
of children.
Nor are the learners
inquired of,
relative to
the curriculum
or the methodology
through which it passes.

We hold
that when instruction
becomes destructive to
the joy of learning—
that instruction
should be abolished
or modified
in such manner
as to lead
potential learners
to experience
the power,
the beauty,
and the magic
of their language.
We pledge allegiance
to the space program,
to past and future
moonshots.
And yes, Virginia
children should have
the Right-to-Read.
A catchy slogan,
unless they also have
the *will* to read
and the *need* to read.

With a firm reliance
on the magic of language
and in the name
of children everywhere,
and by authority
granted us by sundry
teaching certificates,
we mutually pledge
to smuggle language
into reading instruction.